SEEKING REVENGE
FINDING GRACE

SEEKING REVENGE
FINDING
GRACE

From the darkness of Islam
To the light of Christ Jesus

JAMSHID EBRAHIMI

XULON PRESS

Xulon Press
2301 Lucien Way #415
Maitland, FL 32751
407.339.4217
www.xulonpress.com

Paperback ISBN-13: 978-1-6628-4483-6
Ebook ISBN-13: 978-1-6628-4484-3

Introduction

This is a story of a man from the northwest of Iran—or Persia as it was known in the west until the 1930s.

The northwest of Iran in 1950 after World War II was comprised of two provinces, East Azerbaijan and West Azerbaijan. This story takes place in West Azerbaijan in a little town called "Sogolitappeh" (the beloved hill) and is about a boy Jamshid who was born to a man by the name "Moosa" (Moses).

Moosa was born in 1931 during which the country was in turmoil. Iran was coming out of foreign militaries' occupations, and the new king was struggling to keep order in the country.

It is about how God picks up a brokenhearted, abused, and fatherless child and brings him back from the dead after his exposure to anthrax (weapons of mass destruction) and struggles with his childhood and adult life, shapes him up, cleans his wounds, forgives his sins, and makes him His child.

We will read throughout this book how God becomes a father to the fatherless and provides a home for the homeless. **"Father to the fatherless and protector of widows is God in his habitation. God settles the solitary in a home; he leads out the prisoners to prosperity, but the rebellious dwell in a parched land" (Ps. 68:5–6).**

The words of the Bible become a living instruction in a lost man's life.

"Your word is a lamp for my feet, a light on my path" (Ps. 119:105 NIV).

A timid and hopeless young man becomes a spokesman for God. **"He gives strength to the weary and increases the power of the weak" (Isa. 40:29).**

We will see his trials and how the presence of God follows him through those trials. **"When you pass through the waters, I will be with you; and when you pass through the rivers, they will not sweep over you. When you walk through the fire, you will not be burned; the flames will not set you ablaze. For I am the Lord you God, the Holy One of Israel, your Savior" (Isa. 43:2–3 NIV).**

We will see the healing hand of God in his life, how he recovers from the effects of weapons of mass destruction (anthrax gas), internal bleedings, different diseases, and survives refugee life and discrimination through many countries and prospers.

"Surely, he took up our pain and bore our suffering, yet we considered him punished by God, stricken by him, and afflicted. But he was pieced for our transgressions, he was crushed for our iniquities; the punishment that brought us peace was on him and by his wounds we are healed" (Isa. 53:4–5).

We will discover that God is still looking for His lost child to bring him home to bind his wounds, nourish him, and call him His child.

Jamshid was a fanatic Muslim who participated in Islamic teachings and was part of a 20-million army against the Jews, yet in the last second before he was about to commit a murder, killing his uncle to recover his inheritance, he heard a voice that turned his life around. He is half-Kurd from his father's side of the family and half-Turk from his mother's side of the family. The Iranian national language is Farsi, so he spoke Farsi in the school and Turkish and Kurdish at home. In second grade, the school curriculum added the Arabic language to his linguistic skills. In the eighth grade, he was immersed in English language. By the time he finished high school, he spoke five languages, Turkish, Kurdish, Farsi, Arabic, and English. Later in life, before he joined the military, he learned the German language and dropped out of German language school because of the Iran-Iraq war.

You will find that the Lord is the same yesterday, today, and forever. As He led Abraham out from the Ur of Chaldees, the Lord led Jamshid from his home country of Iran to a land that he had never known, and the Lord used this orphan shepherd boy for His glory and honor.

You will discover that the road-to-Damascus experience is not limited to early biblical days, but Jesus still is alive and well to call out His servants from among the unworthy, corrupt, and murderers to glorify His name.

Table of Contents

Chapter One

Early Persian History and Islamic Influence

As a country that bridges the east to the west through the ancient silk road, **Iran** has had significant contribution to other cultures, but the Iranian culture has been an enigma to the people of the Mediterranean civilization and their successors.

The Iranian language has extended into the neighboring countries of Afghanistan(Dari Language) and central Asia, Tajikistan.

Iran has been the source of several religions, such as Zoroastrianism, Manichaeism, Judaism, Armenian Orthodox Christianity, Islam, Baha'i, Yazidis, and even Satanism.

Shia Islam is concentrated in Iran, with a mixture of Sunni Muslims in the south and Kurdish tribes in the northwest.

A Brief Chronology of Iranian History

From 5000 BC to 1000 BC, the Elamites developed an advanced society in southwestern Iran around the city of Susa.

Around 1000 BC, different nomadic tribes speaking different languages settled in Iran. Their culture and economies were based on herding and horses. The Scythians settled in the Northwest in the Zagros Mountains. The Medes settled in the central area, and the Persians settled in the southwest of Iran.

The Achaemenids (Hakhamaneshian) dynasty rose to power from 550–330 BC based on the coalition of Medes and Persians under the leadership of Cyrus the Great. Their empire extended from the western Anatolian lands of the Greeks to the Hindu Kush (currently Afghanistan) in the East.

The Achaemenids established a great empire and civilization, and never before in history had such diverse and distant people with a different language, culture, and ethnicity been brought under one rule and one flag. The big reason for this phenomenon was freedom of religion established by King Cyrus.

The Greeks had resisted the Persians for a long time, fighting for their independence. Philip from Macedonia had gathered a massive army when he fell victim to assassination. His son Alexander led an army of 40,000 men and defeated the Persians in 330 BC, and by 323 BC, he had taken over the Persian empire and died.

After Alexander's death in Babylon in 323 BC, his empire was divided among his generals, and Seleucus took control of Babylon and established the Seleucid dynasty, which ruled Iran until about 250 BC.

In 247 BC, two brothers of Iranian Scythian origin defeated the Seleucids in the northeast of the empire. Arsaces (Arshak; Ask) was a chief of the Parni tribe, from the region between the Caspian and Aral seas. His revolt led to the downfall of the Seleucid empire and the emergence of the Parthian Empire.

At the height of the Parthian Empire, the Parthian emperors began to identify themselves as the descendants of the Achaemenid emperors and Greeks. In AD 224, Ardeshir revolted against the Parthians in the province of Fars and put an end to the Parthian Empire.

Ardeshir, the leader of revolt, claimed descent from a legendary hero, Sassan, and for this reason, the emperors of this dynasty were known as Sassanids (Sassanian). They expanded the empire as large as that of the Achaemenids with the exception of Egypt, Syria, and Asia Minor. They reorganized Iranian bureaucracy for centralization of control, tax reforms, and importation of technology and learning. Zoroastrianism became the state religion. The emperors adopted the title of Shahan shah (The King of Kings). They ruled Iran for 418 years until AD 642 when the Sassanid Empire were defeated by Arab nationalists.

The first caliph of Islam, Abu Bakr, led the Arab army against the Byzantine and Sassanid Empire. First, Damascus was captured from the Byzantines in AD 635. Two years later, Omar's army captured the Sassanid capital of Ctesiphon in the campaign of AD 641–642, and by AD 650, the entire empire was under Arab control.

The Arab conquerors abided by the policy of the religious tolerance of *the people of the book,* adopted from the Sassanid dynasty, such as Jews, Christians, and Zoroastrians, and did not force them to convert to Islam; instead, they put a special tax on the non-Muslims, and it was gradually increased, so it took two centuries for the general population of Iran to become Muslims. Shi'ism started in southern Iraq and spread to Iran but stayed a minority for a long time.

In AD 750, an Arabic group, using an Iranian army, com-
manded by an Iranian general, defeated the Umayyad dynasty
and established the Abbasid dynasty with a new capital in
Bagdad until AD 1000.

By the eleventh century, the leaders of the Oghuz and
Seljuk Turks reached the point of recognition and ruled over
Iran, Iraq, and the Afghanistan area until AD 1220.

In the thirteen century, Genghis Khan with his army of
Turks and Mongols, conquered Iran and much of Eurasia and
remained in power till AD 1501.

The Safavids were an order of Sufis, founded in Ardebil
(Azerbaijan-Iran) in the fourteenth century. They used Turkman
warriors and established a new dynasty in AD 1501.

In the middle of the fifteenth century, the Safavids order
accepted Shi'ism as the true form of Islam, and Iran became
predominantly Shia by the sixteenth century.

In 1524, the Safavids' expansion was stopped by Ottoman
Turks, who were Sunni Muslims. The power of the Safavids
declined, and in AD 1722, Afghans defeated the Safavids and
took their capital city, Tabriz. The Afghans were driven out by
the forces of Afshar tribe and, later, the head of the Afshar
tribe, Nader Shah, conquered Afghanistan, followed by sacking
Delhi. Nader Shah's military campaign exhausted the resources
of Iran, and he was assassinated in 1747 by one of his own
tribal members.

In the aftermath of Nader Shah's assassination, Karim Khan
became the major contender for power and gained control of
central and southern Iran, and by 1760, he had defeated all
of his enemies. Karim Khan opened Iran to foreign influence,
allowing the English East India company to establish a trading
post in Bushehr, the Persian Gulf port. In 1775–1776, he

attacked and captured Basra, the Ottoman port at the mouth of the Persian Gulf, which had diverted much of the trade with India away from Iran.

In 1779, following the civil war and the death of Mohammad Karim khan Zand, the Zand Dynasty ruler of southern Iran, Agha Mohammad Khan, a leader of the Qajar tribe, set out to unify Iran. Agha Mohammad Khan defeated all his rivals and established the Qajar dynasty by 1794. The Qajar dynasty lasted from 1794 to 1925 till the Pahlavi dynasty took over Iran by Reza Shah Pahlavi.

Chapter Two

The New Era of Prosperity

In the aftermath of World War I, there was widespread political unrest against the royalty terms of the British Petroleum concession, under the Anglo-Persian Oil Company (APOC), whereby Persia received 16 percent of net profits. In 1921, after many years of mismanagement under the Qajar dynasty, a coup data took place, and general Reza Khan came to government. By 1923, he had become prime minister and became famous for being an incorrupt leader. On April 25,1925, under his influence, the parliament voted to remove Ahmad Shah Qajar from the throne, and Reza Khan was crowned Reza Shah Pahlavi of the Pahlavi dynasty. Reza Shah modernized the country, and by 1930, he had suppressed all the opposition.

Reza Shah sought to carry out in Iran what **Kemal Ataturk** had done in Turkey. He opened the schools to women and abolished the requirement that women wear chadors (covers). He organized the government and modernized the army. He created a secular judiciary. Reza Shah started a program of redistributing the land by taking some land away from feudal and religious organizations and giving them to the farmers.

Reza Shah tried to weaken the power of the colonial's forces in Iran and succeeded to a higher degree, but at the same time, he needed their technology to modernize the country. ***On March 21, 1935, Reza Shah changed the name of the country from Persia to Iran.***

On August 25, 1941, after the Nazi invasion of the USSR, the British, Commonwealth of Nations' forces, and the Russian army invaded Iran. Reza Shah had declared neutrality in World War II and tried to balance between the two major powers, Britain and Germany. The main reason for the invasion was to secure Iran's oil field and the Iranian railway to deliver supplies to the Russian army.

Reza Shah resisted, and on Sep 16, 1941, he was arrested and deposed and exiled by the British to Mauritius. **Reza Shah's** twenty-two-year-old son, **Mohammad Raza Pahlavi,** became the Shah of Iran, and he signed a treaty with Britain, the United States of America, and Russia, declaring that their military presence was not an occupation, proclaimed Iran as an ally, and Britain, the United States of America, and Russia pledged to withdraw their troops within six months of the end of the war.

Following August 14, 1945, V J Day (Victory over Japan Day) in September 1945, first the United States and then the United Kingdom withdrew their forces within the treaty stipulated period, but the Soviets not only violated the withdrawal deadline; in that time, they had expanded their military power toward the South and set up two pro-Soviet "People's Democratic Republics" within Iranian territory, the Azerbaijan People's Republic, headed by Sayyid Jafar Pishavari, and the Kurdish Republic of Mahabad under Pesheva Qazie Mohammad.

Azerbaijan Democratic Party (ADP) was established in September 1945, headed by Jafar Pishavari, and declared itself to be in control of Iranian Azerbaijan, but after the Soviet troops' withdrawal, Iranian troops entered the region in December 1946, took over Azerbaijan and Pishavari, and his cabinet fled to the Soviet Union.

The Mahabad Republic was led by Qazi Mohammad, the religious leader of Mahabad, backed by Mullah Mostafa Barzani from Iraq, and established KDPI, and Qazi Mohammad was elected the first president of Kurdistan on January 22, 1946. On December 15, 1946, after a long battle between the Iranian army, Barzani Peshmerga, and tribal Kurds, the Iranian military entered Mahabad, officially ending the one-year life of the Kurdish Republic. The Kurdish Republic leaders were tried, sentenced to death, and hanged in Chowar Chira Square in the center of Mahabad in 1947.

In 1949, an assassin attempted to kill the Shah, but he managed to gain power by organizing the Iranian constitution assembly and amending the constitution to increase his power. He established the Senate of Iran, which had been a part of the constitution of 1906 but had never been convened.

In late 1951, Iran's parliament unanimously voted to nationalize Iranian oil and generated a huge wave of nationalism among most Iranians and paved the way for prosperity all over the country until the late 1970s.

The Resilient Nation

Even though Iran was conquered by Arab nationalists and gradually forced to be a Muslim nation, they never gave up their Persian traditions, like celebrating Nowruz (meaning new day) or new year, and Chahar Shanbeh Suri (lit. Festive Wednesday).

Chahar Shanbeh Suri falls on the eve of the last Wednesday of every Persian calendar year, and it is a prelude to Nowruz, which marks the arrival of the spring season on March 21.

Chahar Shanbeh Suri started in the evening with families making a big bonfire in the street or on the rooftops and jumping over the fire, saying, "My yellowness belongs to you, and your redness belongs to me," believing that jumping over fire takes away sickness and negativity and, in return, will fulfill warmth and energy.

On the eve of Chahar Shanbeh Suri, spoon banging is a tradition observed similar to Halloween in the West. People wear disguises, go door to doors, banging spoons against bowls, and receive packaged snacks, trail mixes, and money. In the countryside with flat roofs, people go from rooftop to rooftop, dropping their shawls from the open small skylights and wishing for gifts. People inside the house will tie gifts, money, and candies to the shawl and say, "Pull it up, and may God grant your wishes."

In Azerbaijan, the Azeris make preparations for Nowruz a month ahead and celebrate every Tuesday before the Nowruz. They celebrate four elements of water, fire, earth, and the wind according to Zoroastrian customs.

They clean their house entirely (shaking the house), wash all the clothing and furniture, and purchase new clothing. On the holiday eve, they visit and tend the graves of their relatives and offer sweets and pastries to the people around.

Nowruz is rooted in the Persian religions, such as Mithraism and Zoroastrianism, and it is celebrated among Persians, Kurds, Azeris, Afghans, Albanians, and Tajiks. During Nowruz, people visit friends, families, and neighbors. Visitors are offered tea, pastries, and mixed nuts, and rich elderlies give new notes to young visitors.

My grandfather was an elderly in our town, and many people would come to visit and wish him happy Nowruz. I was the youngest in the family and in charge of serving the guests. It was hard work but rewarding at the same time. The visitors knew my late father and would give me gifts and new notes. That was the best part of the Nowruz for me.

Before the arrival of the Nowruz, families gather around the Haft-sin table and wait for the exact moment of the March equinox to celebrate the new year.

The Haft-sin table includes seven things beginning with the letter S, sin in Farsi:

1. Sabzeh: It is something green—whatever seed that might germinate or grow. Usually wheatgrass;
2. Samanu: This is sweet wheatgrass pudding to symbolize food and wealth;
3. Senjed: It is silver berry, which symbolizes love;
4. Seer: Garlic in English, and symbolizes medicine and taking good care of yourself in the new year;
5. Sib: Apple; usually, a red apple symbolizes health and beauty of the people;
6. Somaq: Sour red berries, used in Persian kitchens, symbolizes the sunrise on a new day; and
7. Serkeh: Is vinegar; it symbolizes growing older, maturing, and gaining wisdom and patience.

Background

By the 1930s, feudalism had lost some power, and some of the farmers, including my grandfather, had received lands for farming on their own rather than toiling for feudal bosses.

My father was born into this environment to a Muslim farmer who had received acreages of lands from the government and had to work the land and make it profitable to pay the government back for the cost of the land. As a young farmer without capital to hire workers to work in the farm, my grandfather relied on his children for labor. He had two daughters before he had his first son who died at a young age. My father Moosa was the fourth child and second son to be born in 1931. Later on, Grandfather had his third son, my uncle.

Moosa, my father, was summoned to the military service from 1952–1954.

He returned home safely at the age of twenty-three and, now, according to the customs, he is a mature man, and he should look for a wife to bear children to be the future workhorses on the farm.

Getting married according to agrarian customs of Iranian Muslims is not just to find someone whom the man is in love with, and he will marry her as a partner for life. No, it is a three-prong act. First, she should be someone the Muslim family knows, trusts, and approves. Second, she should be able-bodied to work in the farm like a workhorse, and, third, she should be able to produce male children (workhorse), and if the first and second criteria are met, and the wife did not produce male children, she will be divorced and replaced with another one.

Chapter Three

My Father's Married Life

Grandfather was from Kurdish background, and Grandmother was Turkish. The Kurds are Sunni Muslim, and the Turks are Shiite. In a tribal society, arranged marriages are very prevalent, so my father's side of the family had arranged my father, Moosa, to marry his cousin (my mother-to-be), Rokhsar.

At the age of twenty-eight, my father got engaged to his cousin Rokhsar, aged thirteen.

My grandfather, being poor and stingy, took advantage of his neighbor's daughter's wedding party and had an engagement party for his son at the neighbor's house and their expense.

He had two daughters, one was married and left the house, and the other one had divorced her husband and came back to her father's house. His first son had died of disease. His third son Parveez was attending school, and he was left with his newly-engaged son working in the newly possessed farm, so Moosa was working the farm, and he was not allowed to visit his fiancée during their engagement.

This sounds cruel but justifiable in Islamic and agrarian society. Because of respect toward parents, children, even in their adulthood, do not have the right to object to their parents' unjust behavior and they simply listen and obey.

Mohammad Reza Shah, the Persian king, had nationalized water sources in Iran and developed canals to farmlands so the farmers can share the water from the canal to water the land.

Each town had a house of justice whose administrator had developed rules and regulations in each small town and had assigned water rights to each farmer based on the size of the farm that the farmer owned. The house of justice's administrator acted as an arbitrator between the farmers if there was a dispute among them.

One day while my father Moosa was watering the farm using water from the canal, he had gotten into a fight with his nephews over who got the watering right on that day, and his nephews had pierced him in the lower abdomen with a pitch fork, perforating his intestines. Moosa was taken to a nearby hospital, and he had recovered from his wounds and was told by his doctor not to lift any heavy object to cause the stitches to rip open and get infected.

Moosa was thirty years when he got married to his cousin Rokhsar in the winter of 1961.

My father did not have any money to his name and was totally dependent on his father for his provision. To get married in Islamic society, the man had to offer a dowry to his bride, plus gifts. My mother was given a set of clothes, a golden bracelet and a golden necklace as gifts. According to my mother, they were happily married for one week when my father was called to work on the farm, and my mother was put to work in the house and the farm.

In Islamic society, a female is a half of a male and a bride in the family is the servant of the rest of the family, and my mother was used as such. Her daily chores were to get up early in the morning, feed the animals, milk the cows, prepare breakfast, set the table for the entire family, clean the table after everybody leaves, clean the house, go to the river, and pitch water for drinking and cooking, which was about two miles both ways. She was to cook lunch, go to the farm, haul animal feed for the animals for the night feed, cook dinner, set and clean the dinner table for the family, and then, if she had any time, she may attend to her husband.

In those days, there was no electricity, running water, or water heater. Farmers and herders used to dig a well in their property, and the water had to be drawn by bucket from the well to water the animals, wash clothes, and take a shower once in a while. My mother had to draw the water from the well and bring wood from Grandfather's lumberyard and heat the water for washing and bathing.

By the end of spring 1961, she was pregnant with her first child, and the workload was increasing daily. Grandmother and Aunty would go to the farm, and my mother would do the house chores.

Grandfather had vineyards, timberlands, wheat farms, and sugar beet farms. He had few workers working for him, but the bulk of the work were on my father's shoulder. My father had to plow the land using bulls or horses six inches at a time, so it would take days and weeks to get the land ready for seeding by hand.

It would take three months of spring and three months of summer for the wheat to ripe and ready for the harvest. The wheat had to be harvested by hand using sickles to cut in the heat of the summer and gathered in sheaves. Then sheaves had to be carried to the threshing field by carriage and be crushed using very primitive tools using rolling blades pulled by animals and winnowed to separate the grain from chaff.

The wheat grain had to be packed in gunny sacks and shipped home by the end of September using horse and carriage. To keep the wheat during the winter, the farmer would dig a deep hole in the ground and bury the wheat for next season also for consumption. The wheat then would be taken to the mill to be crushed and made into flour so the ladies of the household could cook the bread for the family.

As a pregnant woman, my mother was assigned to dig an underground wheat storage the size of 12 x 12 x 8-feet deep on top of the other house chores. She had to dig the dirt using a shovel and haul it by a bucket accomplishing two things; first, prepare an underground storage for the wheat, and second, prepare the dirt for rooftop plastering.

This heavy work had caused her to miscarry her first male child in September 1961. Six months later, in March 1962, she became pregnant again with her second child.

The heavy farm and housework continued to take a toll on my mother and father. After the wheat harvest, since the wheat-crushing was done by a primitive tool, the remaining of the uncrushed wheat had to be carried home and pounded using a wooden bat to crush the wheat shell and make use of the remaining wheat, and that was added to my mother's chores.

On top of the wheat farming, Grandfather had acres of split pea that was harvested and brought home to be crushed by hand and was added to Mother's work load.

Beating wheat and split pea, hours and hours a day with a wooden bat had caused blisters on my mother's hand, and she had no right to complain about it because that would have dishonored the masters of the household, and since she had no right to visit her parents, nobody knew about it, and if or when she was allowed to visit her parents, my grandmother and aunty would accompany her to her parents' house so she would not dare to share anything with anybody.

In Islam, children are considered the property of the parents, and brides of the male children are treated like slaves, and if they complain, they will get in trouble.

One day, our next-door neighbor's wife had visited my mother and noticed the blisters on my mother's hand and asked her; why had she not complained to her father? And my mother responded that she was afraid. So, our neighbor's wife had reported the matter to my maternal grandfather. Grandfather responded to the matter and had come to visit his daughter and asked my mother to show her hands to him, but my mother, beforehand, had poked the blisters on her hand so her father may not find out about it, but Grandfather knew about it because of our neighbor's report and had reported the matter to my paternal grandfather and asked him about mistreatment. But that had made the matter worse, and my mother was mistreated and called a snitch.

Mothers-in-law in Islamic society have a lot of power over house brides. One day, my mother was sent to the vineyard to bring grape leaves to make "Dolme" (stuffed grape leaves with minced meat, rice, and spices), and she had noticed that Grandmother was sitting on the wall watching my mother so she may not eat grapes from the vines. Grandmother was a control freak!

Another day, my father had come home after a twenty-four-hour farm work with torn pants and had asked my mother to sew it for him, so my mother and father had gone to their room to fix his pants. Suddenly, there was a knock on the door demanding that my father should come out and get to work, and it was not the time for intimacy. That was my angry and demanding aunty.

My mother loved my father, and she would prepare a pot of hot water every evening for my father to take a bath, but my father worked twelve hours a day and hardly had any time to take a shower.

Family Feud and Drama

Grandfather was a slave driver and tried hard to get rich fast since he had acquired land from the newly established government, and he was not willing to spend any money on his children and had forgotten his paternal duty toward his children.

Grandmother was bitter upon losing her first son and blamed my grandfather for their son's death, and there was no love lost between them.

Aunty, the first child, was bitter because of being barren and had divorced her first husband and returned home to her father's house. She was angry all the time, bad-mouthing her parents, insulting them, and never got along with anyone. She would even get angry at the chicken's cackling after they had laid eggs and would chase after them and beat them up, saying, "So what, you laid an egg, shut up and get out of here." She was always sour-faced and moody. I called her my emotionally constipated auntie.

My father was a humble man who would not speak back to anyone but took it in the chin and obeyed without question.

My mother, who was in love with my father, would tolerate any abuse for the sake of love.

My second aunty was happily married to a rich relative in a different town. She was the prettiest of the two aunties and had three sons and two daughters. Her husband had a sixth-grade education and read the newspaper every day. He was very arrogant and condescending toward people around him, thought very highly of himself, and walked like a peacock.

My uncle, the younger child of the family, did not care about anything, went along with his school, hardly worked, and he was arrogant and controlling.

Good News in the Family:
A Workhorse Is Born

The time had come for the heartbroken eighteen-year-old young mother, after nine months of pregnancy, a heavy work load, and losing her first child to miscarriage, to give birth to her second child, Jamshid. I was born in December 1962.

Everybody in the family was happy because **another workhorse was born.** My father still carried on the heavy farm work despite the doctor's orders to not lift any heavy load and not much time to spend with his newborn baby. My mother was back to work without much after-birth rest.

A year was past and, according to my mother, I was starting to walk. I was left at home with Grandmother and Aunty, and my mother was gone to farm to bring feed for the animals. On her way back from the farm with animal food on her back nearby my grandfather's house, she noticed my father bent over and could not walk. She asked my father, "What is happening?" and he replied with a fainted voice that he was having massive pain in his lower abdomen. She took my father home and laid him on the bed, and my grandmother, instead of sending him to the hospital, which was only ten miles away, had sent after a lady in the neighborhood who had some medical experience to come. The lady had come and given a hot massage to my father's abdomen.

My mother was told that she needed to go to the farm and bring more food for the animals and was not allowed to provide care for her loved one.

My grandmother burned Esfand seeds around my father to void the evil eye. In Iran, Esfand seeds are used to fight against the evil eye. This is a tradition that has been passed down through generations from the days of **Zoroastrianism.** The idea is to burn Esfand seeds during which time the seeds make a popping sound, then the smoke that comes from the burning seeds must be circled around one's head and home. The smoke and popping sound are said to take away the evil.

A day had passed, and my father's condition had worsened, and my mother was forced to watch her loved one tormented with pain, and nothing serious was done about it. Finally, they had decided to take him to the doctor.

A hard-working farmer who had not taken a shower for weeks, a man who had not shaved for a long time, with patched-up dirty clothes so many times that his shirt looked like a blanket, now laying down on a death bed with no help.

Now, my rich grandfather, embarrassed with his dying son's situation, decided to take off his clothing and put them on his son before taking him to the doctor.

My uncle had taken my father to the hospital. The doctor had examined my father and diagnosed him with a serious lower abdominal infection.

My father had lifted heavy stones to build a wall around my grandfather's vineyard, and the stiches from his previous wounds had opened up, and two days of warm massages had caused a heavy infection in his lower abdomen, developed into peritonitis, had progressed to severe sepsis, and he had died. If they had taken him to the hospital same day, his death could have been avoided.

Chapter Four

An Orphan without Hope

It is 1963, in a small countryside town called Sugolitappeh (Beloved Hill) in the northwest of Iran in the province of West Azerbaijan, we have a seventeen-year-old widow, a one-year-old boy without a father, a dysfunctional family, a grandfather without his workhorse and a lot of leftover farm work, a heartbroken, bitter grandmother who lost two sons, a divorced angry aunty, and a young school-age son who was my uncle.

In Islamic culture (borrowed from Judaism), when a son dies and leaves behind his wife, if there is another son in the family, he should marry his brother's widow to preserve the family's honor and raise his brother's children.

After the death of my father, my maternal grandfather had communicated to my paternal grandfather regarding my mother's marriage to my uncle, but my uncle had refused to do so. To make matters worse, my paternal grandfather, by the advice of my younger aunt's husband, Ismael Khan had gone to court and disowned me as a child and the reason for that was, if I, as a child, would have died for any reason, my mother would have taken the inheritance away and it was done to protect the family inheritance. The greedy aunt's husband had figured out that if one son was eliminated from receiving inheritance, his wife would receive an extra portion of the inheritance after the grandfather's death.

My maternal grandfather sent a message to my father's family, saying "Since there will not be a marriage between my daughter and your younger son, and the child has no inheritance to his name, the only choice left before me is to come and take my daughter away from your house in a week. I will no longer allow my daughter to be your housemaid."

This news had not set well with my family members, and they had opted to retaliate by inquiring about the jewelry they had given to my mother as a wedding gift before her wedding, and they wanted them back. So, they had searched for them in different cabinets, but my mother had sewn a pocket in her undershirt and kept them with her, and anytime my family would ask about the jewelry, she would go to the cabinet, pretend to look for them, take them out of her secret pocket, and show them to my family, and this way, she had managed to retain the jewelry from my father.

The second retaliation was to remove her child from her, even while she was still living in grandfather's house and breastfeeding her child.

I was sixteen months old, still nursing, separated from my mother, hungry and crying, and instead of letting my mother care for me, my aunty had taken over, carrying me around on her back, trying to calm me down.

The bitter moment had come, and my maternal grandfather was at the door of my family with a carriage to load my mother's belongings and take her home. A devastated seventeen-year-old widowed mother, empty-handed with tearful eyes, brokenhearted, blistered hands, infected breasts full of milk, and looking back at her only child had to walk back to her father's house, and my grandmother had broken a black pot behind my mother as to cast a spell on my mother that she may not bear any more sons, and I was left at the mercy of my grandparents and aunty for care.

A Black Goat for a Surrogate Mother

A sixteen-month-old nursing baby, without his mother, now crying, and the frustrated, childless aunty was trying to calm him down. My grandparents doubled down on their greed and arrogance, took revenge on their own relative, cheated her of her right to be a wife to their son and mother to their grandson, and now forced to raise a child with a hateful heart and anguish toward his mother who was not willing to be a slave for the rest of her life.

Restless and without my mother's milk, I had been getting weaker and weaker and had developed severe croup caused by parainfluenza virus. My larynx, trachea, and bronchi were obstructed with inflammation, and I had been coughing and sounding like a seal.

According to my neighbors, I was agitated and cried all the time. So, in their desperation, they asked the next-door neighbor's wife who just had a newborn baby to nurse me, and she had accepted, but she was not available all the time, so they had purchased a black milk goat to feed me with goat milk, hence **my surrogate mother was a black goat.** They kept the goat until I was five years old. Later on, I was introduced to my milk brother and milk mother who were our next-door neighbors, and they loved me a lot. I actually felt he was my real brother.

Sleepless Nights

As a four-year-old child, I remember sleep walking, crying, and getting out of the house at night, and my aunty would wake me up and bring me back to bed. Sometimes I would wake up with a bad cough and could not breathe, and instead of taking me to the doctor in the middle of the night, my aunty would take me to an old lady in town who would use her dirty fingers to clear my airways so I could breathe for a while, and this went on until I was nine years old.

The next day, she would take me to a prayer man so he could write a prayer for me to put me at rest. The prayer man would copy the Quran and write on a long and narrow piece of papers with different ink colors and fold them in a triangle shape, one to pin on my shoulder, one to put under my pillow at night, one to dissolve in water and make me drink, and one to burn under me to void evil. On top of the prayers pinned on one shoulder, they had pinned an evil eye on the other shoulder to cast off the malevolent glare. This went on for another year, and nothing changed.

One day, my aunty took me to another prayer man. The man asked her about me, and she explained the crying and sleep walking. He asked her about my mother, and she replied that my mother was out of my life. This prayer man was not about taking my aunt's money. He said, "There is nothing wrong with the boy; all he needs is his mother. Go in peace." My aunty did not like the answer, and she took my hand and left his office.

The Love of Ali Khan Baba

My great grandfather was a herdsman, and he had few men working for him. Back in those days, jobs were scarce, and most workers stayed with employers from generation to generation and lived like families together. Our next-door neighbor was a man by the name of **Ali Khan Baba** who had worked for my great grandfather, and his three sons worked for my grandfather in the field, and they had known my father and had grown up together. My father had been like a son to Ali Khan Baba, and his death had left a wound in Ali Khan Baba's heart. He loved me a lot to the point that I felt his love toward me more than my own family. My family was so wrapped up in revenge and hatred toward my mother that they forgot to love me or simply did not know how to love. I not only felt his love by his embrace but also saw the love in his eyes. I was very attached to him and his family, and I called him my Alibaba.

His wife would offer me yogurt with a sprinkle of powdered sugar. That was my favorite. He would make bread scoops full of yogurt and offer it to me. Sometimes I would fall asleep in his arms, and he would carry me home. He died of old age when I was four and half years old, and I was devastated. Grandpa gave me the bad news and told me that Alibaba has gone to sleep, and he took me to his funeral.

In Islam after someone dies, the undertaker will wash the corpse in public and prepare the body for burial. I stood by the undertaker as he washed my Alibaba, and I held Alibaba's hand until they took him to the graveyard. I miss Alibaba a lot.

Chapter Five

The Big Lie

On September 1966, one evening before dinner, my uncle sat me on his lap and told me that he was my brother, pointing at Grandfather, saying that he was my father, and pointing at Grandmother, that she was my mother. My uncle was a high-school student, Grandfather was in his early seventies, and Grandmother was in her mid-sixties. As a four-year-old kid, I could not understand, but something deep inside told me that what my uncle was trying to convey to me did not add up. I looked at the neighbors kids whose parents were much younger than mine. I saw their parents hug and kiss them, but my parents were sad and emotionally constipated all the time. I never heard anybody tell me that they loved me. Grandmother used to yell at Grandfather that it was his fault, and Grandfather would shout back, "Shut up," and I had no clue what they were talking about. I was not allowed to ask questions.

**From right to left, me, Grandfather, Grandmother,
and her sister in front of the barn**

Every morning before going to school, my uncle would ask for money, and Grandpa, being a stingy farmer, would deny it, and they always had an argument in the morning.

When my aunty was around, she would take me to the mosque to listen to the Islamic preacher, and once in a while, she would suddenly cover my face, and when I asked why she was covering my face, she would respond that she was trying to keep the flies away. Later on, I found from my mother that my aunty was covering my face so my mother, who was nearby in the mosque, would not see my face.

I was told by my grandmother and aunty that a certain woman, would try to cut my head off, and if any woman approached or tried to give me anything, I should not accept anything and run for my life. One day, I was playing with the next-door neighbors' kids on the street, and a woman approached me, asking how I was doing, and gave me a coin. I looked at her and remembered my grandmother's warning about a certain woman, and with all my might, I threw the coin away and immediately saw tears running down her cheeks, and she went away weeping, and I ran home. Later on, I figured out that she was my mother.

The Days of Enlightenment

In September 1968, they sent me to a school nearby. It was a four-classroom school with five grades. First and second grades were in one classroom, third and fourth grades were in another classroom, the fifth grades in the third classroom, and the school office was held in the fourth room. In our classroom, when the teacher taught first-grade students, second-grade students had to keep quiet and do their homework until the teacher was done with the first grade and vice versa with the second grade.

The school was only half a mile away from our house, and going to school, I would take a shortcut through the next-door neighbor's yard, passing by three other neighbors. People in the neighborhood used to look after me, and they had pity on me. Later on, I found out that everybody new about my situation except me. I was kept in the dark about my past and future. I was told that I was somebody's son, but what I did not know was that I was nobody but an orphan without hope. I was very lonely, depressed, and confused all the time.

On the first day of school, my uncle dropped me off to school and talked to the teachers for me. I was barely five years old. It seemed to me that my family was trying to get rid of me. I felt so little, and I was. My classmates were a head and shoulder taller than me. I was intimidated by the new environment, but my teacher assured me that everything will be fine.

The janitor of the school was a man in his mid-fifties, and he was very nice to me. He took me by the hand to the school office, warmed up my little hands, sharpened my pencil, and brought me to my classroom. After a while, I noticed that I was the only one to receive this much attention, and I questioned him about it, and he replied that he was my grandfather (my mothers' father), and I told him that I have a mother at home, but he said "No, she is your grandmother, your father's mother," and he assured me that everything would be all right.

At home, Grandmother was not motherly. She was depressed, and all she did was sing a sad song and cry. Grandfather had internalized his pain, and he hardly talked. I felt good at the school, but I dragged my feet going home. The environment at home was very gloomy and sad. My only entertainment was to help my grandmother cook, clean, and pick up the eggs from the chicken coop. To make matters worse, that year, we had a big flood, so we packed up what we could and moved in with Grandfather's helper, who lived on higher ground on a hill across our house.

Our little town was located in between the two rivers, and both of the rivers flooded and wiped off everything in between. We lost every building in the property except one. Two months later, during the summer of 1969, Grandfather had the builders rebuild the house and the barns, and we came back home.

Houses in those days were made of two-feet thick mud walls, the roofs were flat with a slight slope for drainage, and there were a few round openings on the ceiling as sky lights. Windows were rare; only rich people's home had windows. Flat roofs had to be plastered with mud mixed with salt and hay to make it waterproof. There was only one door to enter and exit, and it was made of heavy wood. At night, we would barricade the door with a heavy wooden bar to keep the intruders out. For cooking, we had an in-the-wall wood burning stove with a chimney going up through the wall.

For heating, we had in the ground a stove (tandoor) in the middle of the house. Tandoor was a three-feet-wide and four-feet-deep cylinder made of red clay with a combustion air intake on the lower side connected to the floor surface via clay tubes. We used to build fire inside the tandoor using wood and cow dung to warm the walls of the tandoor. Tandoor did not have an exhaust, and during the heating process, we would uncover the skylights to let smoke out, and because of the heavy smoke, the walls of the house would turn dark brown, and every year before the new year, we had to take everything out and whitewash the walls of the house and prepare the house for Nowruz (new year) celebration.

The woman of the house would make thin bread (Lavash) using tandoor hot walls.

To make Lavash, they would make dough by mixing wheat flour, water, yeast, some salt, and letting it rise overnight.

In the morning, they would build fire in the tandoor using wood, cow dung, or anything combustible to heat the walls of the tandoor. After the smoke was cleared, the women of the house would make round balls of the dough, let it sit for ten minutes, flatten it with a roller on a flat wooden base, spread it on an oval shape pad, slap the dough to the walls of the tandoor, and in less than a minute, they would bring out fresh, thin bread called Lavash.

We would put a square table over the tandoor, cover it with a big woolen blanket, and gather around it to keep warm. The table was our dining table, and at night, we slept around it.

For efficiency, we had built our homes side by side and put the stable in between the homes to make use of our animals' body heat. There was a door from the house to the stable for ease of access to milk the cows. In the cold snowy winter, the stable was used as a chicken coop too, so we would collect the eggs without going out of the house. The stable was used as a bathing place because of the body warmth from the animals. The woman of the house would heat water over the tandoor, put a big pan in the stable, and carry the hot water to the stable through the access door so the members of the house could take a shower once or twice a month.

The following year, we had a new and modern school built by the government, and I was registered for second grade. On the first week of school, the education inspector came to our school, and when he entered my classroom, he noticed me and asked how old I was, and I replied, "Six years old, sir." He looked at me and said, "Son, you are too young to be in second grade," and he took me by the hand and put me in the first grade, so I repeated the first grade.

My maternal grandfather was still the janitor of the school, and he put me at the front of the classroom between two girls and told me that they were my aunties, my mother's sisters.

By now, I knew that I had a mother elsewhere, but I did not know why she was not with me.

My aunties would bring goods and sweets from my mother for me, and they would tell me that my mother loved me. I asked my maternal grandfather about my fate, and he told me that it was a long and sad story. All I needed to know that I was loved by them, should listen and obey my father's side of the family, and when I was a grown man, I would find out the rest.

My father's side of the family forbade me from visiting my mother. In Islam, children belong to father's side of the family as property, and mothers do not have any rights.

Once in a while when I was sent out to purchase groceries for the family, I would pass by my mother's house, visit her in secret, and she would hug and kiss me all over for a few minutes. But it did not take a long time for my father's side of the family to find out about it, and they started to question me, and I had to deny it, so they would spy on me, and my visit with my mother was very limited.

At night when I made my bed, I would fold my clothes neatly and put them under my pillow to iron them for the next day, and in the middle of the night, I would notice my aunty searching my pockets to find out if I had received anything from my mother during the day. So, on top of losing my parents, I was always on the lookout for spies, and I was always interrogated about my whereabouts, and that caused me to be a light sleeper.

I was not allowed to play with anyone unless somebody from the family was watching just in case I made contact with my mother.

Grandmother and Grandfather were getting old, Aunty was no longer home to help, my mother had remarried to her next-door neighbor's son, who had a convenience store. Uncle had joined the military for two years, and Grandfather was not happy about it. I was the only workhorse at home. I would get up early in the morning, help pack the beds and put them away, set up the table for breakfast, and clean up before I went to school. Then I would walk a mile to my new school for the morning session from 8 a.m. to 12 p.m., come back home, help Grandmother set the table for lunch and help her clean up, and go back to school for the afternoon session from 2 to 4 p.m.

After school, I would help in cooking, washing dishes, cleaning the house, bringing water for cleaning, bathing, and cooking, attend the animals, do my school homework before I went to bed, and the cycle would begin all over next day.

I picked up where my father had left off, added to it, my mother's chores, plus whatever my aunty used to contribute. Grandmother had lost her interest in housekeeping and hardly ever talked to Grandfather over losing her sons. I was behind on my performance; finally, they had to hire a helper, a daughter of my grandfather's relatives, to help around the house. I was relieved of the house duties and assigned to the stable and farm. We used to have a shepherd boy to help in the farm, but Grandmother kept accusing him of stealing eggs, and he quit.

I finished my second year of first grade with high numbers. My teacher loved me and gave me prizes for being a good student.

I did not have proper care at home and would get sick with a high fever and bad cough, and Grandmother would treat me with suction cups on my back to relieve the fever. In those days, we did not have many clinics or hospitals nor access to medicine. They would treat bad coughs with hookah juice, which was very salty and bitter.

36

One night, I was coughing very bad, and my grandmother gave me some liquid to drink and told me that it was hookah juice. I did not think twice about it, and after I drank it, I found out that nobody in our household smoked hookah. Later on, I discovered that it was her own salty urine and, surprisingly, it calmed down my cough because of the saltiness of the urine.

There were two doctors and one small hospital for nearly 100,000 people, and people were hardly educated. My paternal grandmother was very depressed and angry, and nobody in the household paid attention to her, and she always needed care. One day, I took her to the doctor for her many illnesses. The doctor's office was jam-packed with many patients, we were all sandwiched together, and there was no privacy. A patient in front of us was a Kurdish farm lady who had brought her ill son with severe diarrhea. The boy was very anemic and looked like he had jaundice. The doctor asked the mother about the condition, and she said "Doctor, he has been like this for two weeks, and his stool is very watery, so you can drink it with a spoon." At this, the doctor beat his head with his two hands and was sorry to be a doctor at such a time like that.

The environment at home was very toxic and boring, and I was happy to go to school. **God had not forgotten about me**. Even though I had no access to my mother, but nine months of the year, I was surrounded by my maternal grandfather and my aunties' love and care. I would do most of my homework at the school with my aunties because I did not have much time at home to do so. After school, my aunties and I would help Grandpa clean the classrooms, and I would tag along with my grandpa and aunties to go home so nobody would bully me on the way home.

After school in the summer, my paternal grandfather would take me to the farm and vineyards to help him thin out the grape leaves so the summer sun would ripen the grapes. We would watch over the grapes together at night in September as they were spread to dry, and he would tell me stories of his youth but never answered my question about my father and mother. He had internalized his pain of losing his sons, and he hardly smiled.

As a Muslim, he always prayed, attended mosque, and took me along with him so I could learn the Islamic way of life. He fasted in the month of Ramadhan, paid his Zakat (tenth of his income) to the poor, and kept up with Islamic rule.

In the month of Moharram, the mourning month for the third Imam who was killed by Omayyad tribe over caliphate, we would all attend the mosque and eat food offered to the dead Imam, and after the Mullah's preaching, everybody would line up in two parallel lines. Somebody would chant, and we would repeat after him. One group beat their chests with hands until the skin turned red, yet the other beat their backs with chains until the skin bled, and the third group would shave their heads bald, dress in white, beat their skulls with the side of a dagger until the tops of their heads got numb and, suddenly, they would turn the blade on their heads, crack the skin of their skulls, and blood would splash all over their white clothing to commemorate the death of Imam Hossain, whose head was chopped off, put on a spear, and taken to Yazid the Omayyad. This ceremony separates the Shiite from other Islamic sects. To a non-Shiite and non-Muslim, this ceremony is very demonic, but Shiite Muslims are conditioned, and by going through it, they believe to receive many points toward heaven.

One day, Grandfather asked me to stand behind him and repeat after him to **learn how to pray the Islamic prayer.** He started with the word **Allah O Akbar Allah O Akbar.**

He was a big and tall man. I interrupted him, looked up, and said, "What does that mean, Grandpa?" He replied, "It is the prayer, and you are supposed to repeat after me and do not ask question." I asked him, "What language is that?" He said, "It is Arabic, God's language. He is the God of Arabs, and we are Muslims."

This left me very puzzled. How come a Kurdish/ Turkish man prays in the Arabic language, a language that he does not understand, and call it worship? What kind of God is this who is limited only to one language for communication with his creation? I kept questioning Grandpa time after time. Finally, he said, "Son, we are Muslims by the force of the sword, not by our own will. Our ancestors were Zoroastrians, and in the seventh century, we were forced to become Muslims."

He taught me how to work hard and showed me the skills of farming and vine dressing. Looking back, I think he knew that the hard work and art of farming would be my only inheritance, and I am still grateful for that.

I used to watch my grandmother sitting at the edge of the yard, staring at the hill across our house, where her sons were buried, and weeping, and when she would see me coming, she would immediately stop and pretend to do something.

In September 1970, I was registered for second grade. My teacher was aware of my life story, and my grandfather sat me in between the two aunties on the front seat, so I had the protection of my aunties and my teacher from the teasers in the school. I cherished every moment of time with my aunties. One day, my aunty brought me some pastry from my mother. I was enjoying my mother's pastry when my classmate and next-door neighbor Hossein approached me and asked for some pastry. I refused, and he chased after me, so I shoved the rest of the pastry in my mouth and choked, almost suffocating, and there was my sweet aunty who pulled the pastry out of my throat and saved my life.

In the second grade, Persian education system introduced a portion of the Quran's small chapters to study. And I was so excited that I would finally get to study the God of Islam's language, the Arabic language. I studied hard and mastered it, and Grandpa was proud of me. I would wash up with Grandpa, pray along, and tell him the meaning of it, and he loved it. From that point on, I made the reading and understanding of the Quran my daily practice.

Iran was prospering, and the Shah of Iran modernized the country, and the tractor and other mechanized tools were available to the farmers. So, Grandfather did not need as many laborers as before. He used the tractor to plow and seed the ground. He used the combine harvester to harvest the wheat and split peas. The tractor was very essential in planting and harvesting sugar beet and transporting it to the sugar factory.

Because of the introduction of fertilizer and pesticides, he managed to have better crops and prospered. The diseases were being irradicated, Malaria was under control, and we were all given a hydroxychloroquine treatment. We all got our measles vaccine, and the life expectancy increased.

My second grade went well, and I gained confidence. My aunty (Father's sister) remarried, and we had semi-peace in the house. Uncle was discharged from the military and was hired as a fifth-grade teacher in my primary school, and they bought me my first suit.

With Uncle back, we had a new boss in the house. He used Grandfather's resources, demolished my father's bedroom from which they all had bad memories, and built a new, modern brick house, presumably for himself. He had a brickmaker take the dirt from the yard and make bricks. As a result, we had a big lower front yard, so he turned it into a garden and orchard. He built a new front iron gate, paved the front yard, and bought himself a car, and I thought he was doing it for all of us, not to mention that he had the power of attorney and was in charge of Grandfather's assets.

Neighbors and the town people, when they saw me work my tail off, would tell me that I have been disowned by my grandfather. I had no inheritance in the family, and I should not kill myself for them, and when I questioned my grandfather, he would deny it and call the people names.

One day, I had a small window of opportunity to look through the legal papers to find the truth, and I came across Grandfather's birth certificate, and on the second page of his birth certificate, I found that my father's name was eliminated from the list of his children, and my name was nowhere to be found.

I shared this with my maternal grandfather, and he said that was true, but I need to be wise and put up with it until I finished my high school and military service, then I could claim my inheritance, but there was a slim chance because my paternal grandfather had disowned me legally, and unless he declared me as his son, I would not receive anything, and this was the beginning of a bigger disappointment on top of being an orphan.

This was my maternal grandfather's advice: "Work hard; it will make you stronger. Study hard; it will make you smarter. Obey your elders; it is God's commandment.

I started the third grade with more knowledge about my past and future. My father's side of the family kept lying to me that I was their son to keep me working as a slave.

Uncle, being the first educated member of the family, was a dictator. One summer, I was sent to keep watch over the vineyard, and from the shack, I saw a wolf. I was afraid and ran away to my grandfather in the threshing field, and my uncle was there. He asked why I ran away, and I told him about the wolf. Instead of helping to overcome my fear, he slapped me and sent me back to the vineyard.

He never tried to help me in my studies nor would he encourage me, but he always made sure that I feared and obeyed him. He always acted as a member of mob, very disrespectful of the others, and thought very highly of himself, so nobody could carry a conversation with him. One thing he could not avoid was to make sure I dressed fine to keep the appearance of me being taken care of by them.

Every day, I had to set up the table, cut fresh vegetables from the garden, clean and wash them, dish the food, and, if by chance, a salt shaker was missing from the table, he would throw a fit and yell and scream at me. Sometimes Grandfather would try to defend me, and Uncle would walk away from the table and leave the house.

In fourth grade, I was fortunate to have a hometown gentleman who was a distant relative of my maternal grandfather as my teacher. He knew my father and treated me well, and gave me the incentive to study hard. I was his number-one student. My teacher was also the school principal, and anytime if there was a missing teacher due to illness or family issues, he would send me to that teacher's class to teach.

**This is me on the first day of second grade.
My second-grade teacher took this photo.**

In the summer of 1972, my maternal grandparents went to the City of Mashhad for a Shiite pilgrimage. This is the sixth Imam of Shiite Muslims, Imam Reza, who was poisoned to death with grapes by Haroon Al Rashid, Abbasid. They had buried him in the City of Mashhad and built a mausoleum for him, and people would go and worship him; hence, the Shiite religion is called a dead-worshiping religion.

When they returned from their pilgrimage, they had purchased a raincoat for me. Everybody in town knew that they are back because of the ceremonial return from the holy city. One day, there was a knock on the door, and when I opened the door, I was shocked to see my grandparents at the door, so I informed my paternal grandfather of it and, surprisingly, he invited them in.

Since there was no relation between the two families, I did not know what to do, be happy or sad. But suddenly, they all started weeping in a loud voice. It took a while before they calmed down. Looking back, I understood that both parties were feeling guilty of their past, but it was my mother's family who extended the peace offering and brought me a gift, and I loved that raincoat.

In 1973, the fifth grade was a milestone in modern Iran because students take a national exam and receive a certificate of accomplishment to enter the job market. My uncle was my teacher, and I did good, but the hard part was that my maternal grandfather, the janitor of the school, had put me in front of the class between my two aunties, and my uncle did not like it, but he had to put up with it.

I loved to read books. It was the tenth anniversary of **White Revolution** in Iran, led by Mohammad Reza Shah, the Iranian king in 1963. I had studied it well and wrote my first essay and read it publicly. My competition was my aunty, but we got along well. The White Revolution modernized Iran by building schools, health clinics in every town, main highways between the cities, strong military, universities, factories, land distribution, forest nationalization, profit sharing among industrial workers, and water resource nationalization.

The Shah named it the White Revolution because it was bloodless. The revolution made peasantry happy because the Shah bought the land from landlords and sold it at a lower price to the citizenry; at the same time, it made the landlords angry. The second angry group was the powerful Shi ah clergy, whose traditional powers were removed because of education and changes in family laws; also, a large percentage of clergy came from landowning families. So even though **White Revolution,** overall, was beneficial to the country, it had its archenemies that eventually resulted in the **Red/Islamic Revolution,** led by the clergy in 1979, and the Shah was forced out.

Because of the national exam, we had to take a picture for the certificate, and all of us fifth graders had to go to town to a photographer to have our pictures taken, and the janitor, my maternal grandfather, was in charge of that.

He took us to the city called Miandoab, meaning between two rivers because the city was located between two rivers of Simeenehrood and Zarrinehrood. It was an exciting time for all of us. Not only did we get to see the glamor of the city but also, he took us for an ice-cream treat.

Despite the nightmares and family dysfunctions, I passed the national test with a B-plus grade.

In 1974, I attended middle school (sixth to eight grade) in the city of Miandoab, a ten-mile distance from the family home. It was the first year, thanks to the White Revolution, that we had asphalt road to travel on. I traveled on a bicycle with several classmates from our little town. It was a bigger school and intimidating. City boys picked on us, but it did not stop me from getting to the top of the class. I **excelled in Arabic and my religious studies.**

I always remembered my maternal grandfather's advice to study hard. During the summer, I would get a set of used books for the following grade and studied ahead of time while watching the vineyard. I always had an answer for the question in the classroom. Sometimes I would answer the question asked of someone else, and I would get in trouble with my teacher, and he would send me out of the classroom as punishment.

I was quiet and polite, and my teachers loved me. One day, I was sick with croup again and stayed home; the school had a combined two-classrooms study, and there was a geography quiz that nobody had an answer for it, and my teacher had been looking for answer and had said, "Where is Jamshid when I need him?"

My family met my physical needs, but emotionally, I was always down, but **God had not forgotten me.** The school principal recognized me by my last name and said that he was my father's teacher. So, **the Lord had another set of eyes on me.**

At home, Grandmother was more depressed and sought attention from family members, and she had to be taken to the doctors more often. Uncle was looking for a wife. He was a teacher, and there was no highly educated female in town to marry. The government purchased a piece of land from my paternal grandfather and built a school for girls, and the teachers of the school were females, and my uncle had his eye on one of them, but he had competition, the next-door neighbor's son, who was my uncle's classmate.

One summer evening, we were sitting at home and waiting for Uncle to show up for supper, and suddenly he showed up badly beaten by his competitor and his brothers over that female teacher in the school. They had not left any sign of injury except they had pulled his hair off, and my uncle could not sue them, but by the advice of his nephew, he stabbed himself with a kitchen knife and sued the next-door neighbor's sons and sent them to jail. Eventually, by the advice of the town council, they reconciled, the neighbor's sons were released, and Uncle married that girl.

In 1975, I continued in the same middle school in seventh grade. At home, I had to do most of the cooking, cleaning, gardening, and taking care of my grandparents.

Grandfather sold all of the animals because there were no more workers to hire for low wage. The industry was booming, and the towns were emptied of laborers. More and more people owned cars, and the construction activities were increasing. There was more mechanized farming than before, and the farmers were more prosperous.

Iran now had a strong military. F14 jets, purchased from America, were flying all over the country for show of strength. The Iranian military was well trained by the Americans and was equipped with American top-notch military supplies.

Saddam Hussein, the president of Iraq, launched an attack on the Western Iranian border with his tanks columns and was easily defeated by the Iranian army.

The Iranian air force, backed by Americans, was able to disable Iraqi radar, and Iranian F14 had invaded Iraqi sky over Bagdad, and Saddam Hussein pulled his troops back and accepted defeat.

I was the envy of the rich city boys because of my hard work in the school. One day, as I prepared for my test in the school ground during the break, I was suddenly hit on my legs with a chain. I turned around and saw a short city boy, and I asked him the reason for hitting me. He said he liked it that way, and asked what I was going to do about it. I, being a clean freak, slowly put my study book aside, took my jacket off and put it away, and being a strong cowboy, grabbed his shoulders and spun him around me several times and let him fly. It was a rough, gravely ground he skidded on facedown. He had all kinds of bruises on his belly and face. I simply went over and sat on his back and did not let him move.

The school kids were gathered around, shouting, "**Bully is down, bully is down,**" and I felt a tap on my shoulder, calling my name. I looked up; it was the school principal. So, I let the boy go. He had to be taken to the school clinic to attend to his wounds. I was questioned by the school principal, and when I showed him the chain marks on my legs, he let me go, and it was justified as self-defense. That was the end of bullying on the school ground, and the city boys did not bother me anymore.

1976 was my eighth-grade year, the year of prosperity in Iran. The Shah had implemented a school lunch program, and we received food and fruits on our school breaks. The fruits were from Israel and were delicious and healthy. I had my yearly new suit, and I mostly had the same teachers.

Grandmother's health deteriorated. I was doing well on my first-semester exams. But on my science exam, Grandmother checked into the hospital for overnight observation, and Uncle put me in charge, so I could not study. The next day during the exam, I had the answers right by 85 percent, but I was in competition with another student, so I cheated and got caught by my favorite teacher, and he failed me. Had I left it at 85 percent, I still could have been on top because my competition did worse.

I pleaded with my science teacher's wife, who was my English teacher, for mercy, but it did not go anywhere. He said that he wanted to teach me a lesson and, boy, I learned my lesson all right. I never repeated that again. Eventually, I caught up with my grades, recovered, and learned from my mistakes.

It was September 1977 that I started my first year of high school. I had a new full-size bicycle and new suit for the year. The school was in the middle of the town, and I did not like the traffic. The police officers were corrupt and expected bribes. One day, I parked my bicycle and went into the bookstore to buy a dictionary. When I came out, the police officer stopped me and tried to deflate my bicycle tires for being on the pedestrian way, but thank God for my English teacher who was passing by and stopped him; otherwise, I would have had to walk home and drag my bicycle with me.

In the spring break of 1977, my prosperous uncle decided to take the whole family for a pilgrimage to the city of Mashhad and visit the sixth holy Imam's grave. He had a three-passenger car. His wife sat in the front seat and Grandpa, Grandma, aunty and I were sandwiched at the backseat, and we traveled one thousand miles to the holy city.

I was brought up a Shiite Muslim and believed in the traditions of Islam but visiting a grave of an Arab who had died centuries ago did not make sense to me, and I was puzzled on how an educated uncle would believe such a thing, but I digress.

I had experience visiting my father's grave once a year, and I had tried to communicate with him but to no avail, and I did not expect anything from this dead Arab either.

We found a home to rent for twelve days. During the day, we would go to the Mausoleum and visit the graveside. The grave was inside a big mosque with golden minaret, dome, and gates. Inside the mosque, the grave was surrounded with golden bars and a small golden gate, and behind the bars, I could not see the grave because it was covered with money and jewelry of naïve people who had offered their money and livelihood to receive a blessing in return from a dead man.

My silly aunty took off her jewelry and threw them inside the grave, wishing for a husband and, surprisingly, she got one. But she could never get along with any husband and could not keep them. She had married three times and divorced them one after another. She died at her father's house without one.

Inside the mosque, it was very congested. People were sandwiched against each other, and it was very muggy and smelly, so the mosque authorities had installed rosewater pumps that would spray rosewater over the crowed to keep the air somewhat fresh. We managed to take my grandparents to the bars of the grave, and they kissed the golden bars.

I just watched in awe at the depth of demonic deception, and I saw sick and demon-possessed people tied up to the golden gates of the mosque, hoping for healing from a dead Arab man who had not contributed anything to the Persian culture except destruction. The Shiite Muslims would sell their crops and animals to take on their pilgrimage under the guise of gaining points toward entering heaven, and in the process, some would lose their lives by being trampled on or in an accident while traveling by bus or train.

Overall, it was a good trip for me. I got to see the northern part of Iran, enjoyed good food and pastries, and I used my savings and bought my first Russian camera.

Chapter Six

Islamic Revolution

On October 1977, civil unrest began between Khomeini supporters and Shah's government, and it intensified toward the end of the school year. I did good with all the subjects except geometry, and I had to take summer class to catch up.

The country was totally divided, even among Muslims. There were many factions, but people were united against arbitrary rule implemented by Shah (the king) and westernization of the country, where American diplomats and agencies were immune from any prosecution. People were already sick and tired of foreign influence of the past, such as Russia and Britain, and they could not take it anymore. Khomeini used those hostilities to unite the country under the name of Islam for his benefit.

In the summer of 1978, as a result of Rex Cinema burning in the city of Abadan in the southwest of Iran, in which 422 people burned alive, the revolutionaries blamed the Shah for it and took it to the streets. Later on, a lone wolf admitted that he did it as an ultimate sacrifice for the revolutionary cause, but the Islamic government executed him for the setting of the fire by order of the Shah.

In the second year of high school in September 1978, I changed my school to another high school at the edge of the town, away from police officers and traffic. The school principal was a hometown gentleman and distant relative who was my father's classmate at one point, and he liked me. **And the Lord had not forgotten this orphan boy.** The principal watched over me.

The situation in the school was very intense. Strikes and demonstrations paralyzed the entire country. There were shortages of food and supplies all over the country. The students would go to school not to study but to organize and take it to the streets for demonstrations against the Shah's regime. The Iranian military defended the regime against demonstrators all over the country, and many died as a result.

I had a choice to make, attend the demonstration or go to Grandfather's farm and work. I went to the school principal who was a devout Muslim, and he advised me to go home using the back door of the school. He said there was too much politics, hatred and little of Islam. Knowing these as the background for the Islamic revolution, I refused to attend a demonstration but devoted to the Islamic teachings.

Three things that were influential in Shah's demise:

1. The Shah's land reform benefitted many farmers but not everybody; therefore, it left behind an agitated peasantry without land who were used by Khomeini against the Shah;

2. The Shah's support for OPEC, instructing OPEC countries to reduce the oil production; therefore, an increase in oil price cost him loss of support from the West, even though he was considered a puppet of the West by the majority of Muslims in Iran; and

3. Family law reforms and secularization of the court systems that took away the power of the clergy in rural areas, on top of the land reform that took lands from the rich clergies; therefore, the clergy had utmost hatred for Shah.

The Shah appeared on national television, admitting his shortcomings, asking for forgiveness, giving a short report of his many achievements for the country, and warning his countrymen to take care of their country against the foreign invasion.

Knowing he was suffering from cancer, he mentioned he would be taking only a box full of Iranian soil to lay his head on when he was ready to die. He left Iran, along with his family, in exile, on January 16, 1979, as the last Persian monarch.

On February 1, 1979, Khomeini arrived in Tehran with overwhelming support of agitated Iranians and, shortly after, on February 11, 1979, the revolutionary guerrillas overcame the loyal troops to the Shah and established the Islamic army called Pasdaran, comprised of cowboys and peasantries who were after power and money.

Iranians voted by national referendum to become the Islamic Republic of Iran on April 1979, establishing a theocratic-republican constitution.

The Iranian army declared neutrality and stopped shooting at the demonstrators. The new government was established by the order of the Rohullah Khomeini, the new revolutionary leader. The members of the new government consisted of religious leaders, and many opposition party members against the Shah with many different points of views added insult to injury, to say the least. This created an unstable leadership in the country, and we ended up having too many chiefs with few Indians. The majority, even though, united against the Shah, but were extremely divided against each other.

Islam, from its origin, has been using the strategy of divide and conquer by its founder Mohammad, the prophet of Islam, to take control of the masses, and now they succeeded in a major way in conquering Persia for a second time in history and destroying its foundation.

The Kurdish people used the chaotic situation to declare Kurdistan an independent country for the second time. The Kurdish peshmergas, armed with AK-47 guns and ammunitions stolen from the military bases during Islamic revolution, started attacking nearby villages to add to their territory. The totally disorganized, untrained Pasdaran Islamic army felt obligated to defend the country against Kurdish freedom fighters against whom they were no match while the national army stayed neutral.

My high school philosophy teacher, who was a very nice gentleman and a devout Muslim, joined the Islamic army against the Kurdish freedom fighters. During the fight, he was taken hostage. The Kurds had identified him as a fanatic Islamic philosophy teacher. They had pulled his teeth and cut off his tongue before boiling him alive in a big pot of tar until his body shrunk to the size of an infant, and then delivered his charred body to his family through a third party in exchange for Kurdish freedom fighters who were taken hostage by Islamic military.

One of my Kurdish relatives joined the peshmergas. He was a brave fighter and took over the leadership of a peshmerga battalion. One night, he and his comrades had attacked the Islamic army camp on a mountain top and killed almost everyone, then my relative decided to go into every tent and finish off everyone who was alive. As he entered the last tent, one young Islamic soldier taking his last breath had aimed his rifle to the tent entrance, and as my relative entered the tent to finish him off, he shot and killed my relative. His death was a great loss to the Peshmergas, and the news spread to every Kurdish camp. The Kurds attacked several Islamic watchtowers and took twelve Islamic soldiers captives. They had a huge funeral for my relative, and after his burial, they slaughtered the twelve Islamic soldiers and shed their blood over his grave as a sacrifice for revenge.

After that event, the Kurds decided to take over the city of Miandoab (the city between two rivers), passing by my little town on foot. I still remember watching peshmergas through the window of our house, as though I was watching a war movie as they leaped like a mountain goat with their AK-47 in their hands.

The Islamic army had their post on top of the hill across from our house, and as peshmergas approached, they left their barracks and retreated toward the city. The peshmergas proceeded with full force toward the city, led by a Kurdish general. The Islamic army created a barricade five miles before the city, hid under the road bridge, and slowed down the Kurdish freedom fighters. At that point, the fearless general had come down from his vehicle to check and see the reason for the slowdown, and one of the young Islamic army soldiers had jumped out from under the bridge and shot the general point blank and killed him on the spot. The Kurds killed the Islamic soldier and his companions, but their attack was halted because of lack of leadership.

With Kurdish peshmergas around, we packed our valuables and moved in with my married auntie in another town for safety twenty miles away. We had small handguns that were no match to Kurdish machine guns and trained fighters.

With all these commotions, my school activities were limited to a few hours a day, and at the end of the year, we only studied less than half of the subjects that resulted in an academic decline for all the students.

I still kept my grades high and entered my sophomore year in 1979 in the same school but different setup. The Islamic government immediately changed the school curriculum, changed the history books and many definitions in our studies, cut down the sizes of the books, and caused further decline in academic growth. The school tuition was no longer free. The school lunch program was eliminated.

All of the foreign professors left the country along with the brain powers of native Iranians who left the country for better and free life. Many manufactures were destroyed and closed.

They killed military officers, looted business, and confiscated Jews, Christians, and Baha'i properties. Baha'i people were burned alive on the streets, and this caused a mass migration of brain powers, business people, and educators from Iran. It was a massive loss for Iran and a big gain for the West. The revolutionaries arrested Prime Minster Hoveida, tried him in Islamic kangaroo court, and killed him.

The production of goods and services were down, Iranian currency lost its value, and Iranians faced stagflation. The government, if you could call it so, rationed food and instituted food coupons, and people had to line up for food and gasoline. Jobs became scarce, incomes declined, and taxes were implemented on people and businesses. Education was no longer free, young adults could not afford to get married, prostitution became rampant, constitution and secular laws were changed, Sharia laws became the governing laws of the land, real Islam was in control of the country, and the clergy got their power back.

The masses who thought by revolting against the old regime's corruption and removing the Shah would have a clean slate and a just government were now having buyer's remorse, and corruption increased exponentially. With the old regime, people could oppose its corruption and spent time in jail, but the new regime, if they dared to oppose, they would lose their lives.

One day, early in the morning hour in the city of Tabriz, the capital of East Azerbaijan, people were lined up for fresh bread, and a villager on his carriage pulled by a donkey was passing by, delivering goods. Seeing the crowd, his donkey got excited, started braying, and startled the sleepy crowd. An old sober man broke away from the crowd and ran to the donkey, grabbing hold of the donkey's jaws, saying, "Keep quiet. We brayed once, now we have to line up for our bread; if you keep braying, you, too, have to stay in line for your barley to eat."

In September 1980, my senior year of high school, they changed our high school's name from Pahlavi to Ali Shariati and our school books. Uncertain of school outcome with colleges and universities closed, I continued and finished my high school.

With every educational institute shut down, I decided to take a detour and convinced my family to send me to Germany, so I could get an education. I signed up to learn the German language at Goethe Institute in Tehran, interpreted my high school diploma, and applied for acceptance from German universities. Everything was in place, and I only had to finish my language school and move on with my plans to become a doctor.

Just in the middle of my language school, Saddam Hussein attacked Iran on September 22, 1980. I was on my way home for the weekend from Tehran to Miandoab, taking a bus nearby Tehran International Airport when I saw Iraqi Migs attack the airport, and an airplane engulfed in fire, and by the time I arrived in Tabriz, I noticed the Tabriz oil refinery on fire.

All eligible adults over eighteen years old had to join the military, train for three months, and go to war. The Iranian military was in disarray. Heads of the Iranian military were executed by the Islamic regime or were exiled. The military and air force supplies were cut off because of a discontinued relationship with America who was the main supplier of military equipment, so the Iranian war machine was like a turtle trapped in the mud.

In a very short time, Iraqi armies invaded Western Iran, and Iranian troops were taken by surprise and retreated. The origin of the war was over a number of territorial and political disputes between the two countries.

Iraq wanted to seize control of rich oil-producing areas of Iran called Khuzestan, and the banks of Shatt al Arab, a river formed by confluence of the Tigris and Euphrates rivers that was the border between the two countries. Saddam was also concerned about Islamic revolution in Iran that could influence the Iraqi Shia majority to incite rebellion in Iraq.

In September 1980, the Iraqi army captured Khorramshahr, but it could not take over the biggest oil refinery in Abadan, and, eventually, the refinery was destroyed by artilleries and cost millions of dollars to repair it. Iran recaptured Khorramshahr in 1982.

Many of my classmates and neighbors were summoned to the military, died, and came back in body bags. One day, as I was managing our lime factory outside of our little town, I saw my classmate Hossein wave at me as he drove his farm tractor heading toward a Kurdish town nearby. Half an hour later, I saw him hitchhiking home. He approached me, and after some family news exchange, he asked me to give him a ride home on my motorcycle, and I did.

He was married to my employee's sister and had a beautiful daughter.

When we arrived to his house, he mentioned that he sold his tractor to provide for his family and would be joining the military, and he already missed his wife and daughter, and he added that he would not make it back home in one piece. A week later, he joined the military, and three months later, he was deployed to Southwest Iran to the border of Iran-Iraq.

Hossein was a fighter all during our school days, but on that day at the front line of the war, he had lost control of himself and instead of laying down behind the barricade, he had panicked, started running, and was machine-gunned and killed by Iraqis. His daughter was raised by his mother, and his high school philosophy teacher from another town married his wife.

To keep safe, thinking that the war would be over soon, I stayed back from the military and worked at Grandfather's farm, but we were not safe back home either.

We lived at the border of Kurdistan and Azerbaijan by the river. There was constant fight between Kurdish freedom fighters and the Islamic army, and we had farms by the river.

One day, I was watering the family farm by the river, and I had my shovel on my shoulder while walking on the farm. The Islamic army on the hill ten miles away, watching with binoculars, thought that I was a Kurdish freedom fighter and carrying an RPG (rocket-propelled grenade) on my shoulder on this side of the border. Suddenly, I heard the fifty-caliber bullets flying around me. I immediately went down flat on my face, hid behind the tall grass, and waited till dark to go home to avoid being shot, and I was saved. **The Lord was there, and I did not know it.**

The next summer, because of the heavy work load, my family purchased a motorcycle for work so I could get more accomplished. I was dressed in Kurdish attire, which was looser and more comfortable, riding my motorcycle to work, not too far from the Kurdish border. The Islamic army had been hiding in the bushes so they could ambush Kurdish freedom fighters. They had thought that I was a Kurdish freedom fighter, and they had me on their crosshairs with their RPG, but I stopped to check on the other piece of land. I saw them running toward me with their loaded riffles; when they saw me, they were happy that I had stopped and told me that God had mercy on me; if I had not stopped, they would have shot me with an RPG, and **I found out for sure that the Lord was with me.**

Chapter Seven

The Soldier

As an Iranian without military cards, no one could enter the workforce, attend any educational faculty, or even get a passport. I had to make a decision; take the risk of dying and get my military card with a 50/50 chance of survival or work as a slave for Uncle.

Uncle had figured out that as long as there was a fear of dying, I would not join the military to get my cards and be a man of my own, and I would be working for him for a long time. He had made sure that I had no bank account of my own by checking with all the banks in the neighborhood, and even tried to hook me up with one of his sisters-in-law just to make me his own personal slave.

I had no inheritance in the family and without military cards, I had no future in the country nor could I leave the country.

I joined the military on January 14, 1984, without telling my family. On that day at the recruitment center, I came across my neighbor's son, who was two years younger than me. His father had served the country with my father. He was happy to see me there for moral support. We sat next to each other on the bus, going to boot camp. He was a hard-working farmer, young hunter, and sharp shooter but did not have enough life experience. He told me that his father was heartbroken to see him join the military in time of war, but being with me would give his father some peace of mind.

He was afraid for his life and said that he would not come home alive. I encouraged him and later on promised his father to watch over his son.

After three months of training in **Shahrood** boot camp in Central Iran in a minus fifteen-degree Fahrenheit climate, where many of the young soldiers came down with hypothermia and were hospitalized, I was assigned to the **Battalion Strength Combat Engineering** unit in **Boroojerd**. I had no clue what that was except it sounded very fancy and technical until I found out that we would be **constructing pontoon (floating) bridges** over the war zone rivers, serving as a **sapper** (a military specialist in field fortification work and demolition), deploying and deactivating explosive chargers and unexploded ammunitions, mapmaking, camouflage, and a wide variety of construction services supporting frontline troops, not to mention operating .30 cal. and .50 cal. machine guns, anti-tank rockets, and grenade launching.

To be honest, even as a Muslim, I had no desire to die because this war was not the war of our choosing nor was it an Islamic war. I had to think fast, and I did.

As soon as we arrived to our unit, I found out that my typing and archiving skills could come handy and told the officer in charge of individual assignments that I was an archivist and typist, and I ended up doing that.

ZPU 4, Four-barreled towed anti-aircraft gun

Land mine training

Main Military Office as typist and Archivist

I was assigned to the main military office and performed typing military letters, archiving, and printing the weekly military report. I organized the archiving office better than the officers who were trained for that purpose, and I got two promotions in the span of one year. My unit commanding officer did not like my ethnicity and assigned me to the frontline office in-war zone. I packed up and reported to the frontline office in the war zone the next day, twenty miles behind enemy lines in Southwest Iran called **Khuzestan.**

Typing in an underground war zone office

We went through another round of defensive and offensive training, how to build underground bunkers against incoming bomb shells, what to do in case of chemical attacks, such as mustard gas or anthrax. We were trained on how to use atropine auto injectors and wear masks in case of biological weapons used by the Iraqi army. Atropine is used as an antidote against neurological gases.

My neighbor's son was assigned to the frontline army, and they were losing hundreds of foot soldiers a day. To keep my promise to his father, I contacted one of the relatives on my mother's side, who was in an upper echelon of military and asked for his help in protecting my friend. He was a major in the army, had served with many generals, and was Shah's personal guard while Shah was in Iran. He contacted my friend's commanding officer and made sure that my friend got an easy assignment. My friend was put in charge of generator operation and maintenance, and I had a sigh of relief that I kept my promise to his father, and my friend was safe.

It was April 1985 in the Southwest Oilfield desert. There was no vegetation, no water, snakes and scorpions were everywhere, and all we could see were mirages and a flat oil field. The average day time temperature was ninety degrees Fahrenheit, and at night, it would drop down to the forties.

Our water supply came from the muddy **Karun River.** All of us developed kidney stones and had to be treated. Some of us resorted to drink nonalcoholic beer to dissolve the stones.

Our shower stall was five feet by five feet, made of corrugated sheet metal in the open field without a shelter with a showerhead connected to a water tank. Where to run and hide during an Iraqi air or ground attack while in the shower was a million-dollar question.

Our bathroom was a real outhouse in the open without any protection from bombshells. It was made of corrugated sheet metal, and the sewer ran into an open field, which was a big hole in the ground

In the heat of the summer, it stunk bad, and the military had dropped a low voltage electric cord into the sewer to kill the bacteria and microbes. Flies were everywhere, and we did not have any defense against them.

Due to constant Iraqi artillery attacks, our bathroom breaks were very short and concise. We would take the bathroom breaks only when it was very urgent.

I worked in an underground bunker along with the war commanders and generals and, yes, I was a war secretary where I used to get the raw news.

Iranian military was very racially diverse. Kurds did not like Turks and Persians hated both Kurds and Turks and called them names. Officers of different races discriminated against other race soldiers and officers. Sexual abuse was rampant, and if the soldier dared to resist, the abusing officer would assign the soldier to the front line to be slaughtered by Saddam Hussein's army.

I am half-Turk and half-Kurd and educated among Persians, so I got along well with everybody. We had a Kurdish lieutenant general, and he did not like me mixing with Turks and Persians. One day during morning exercise, I was slapped from behind by a Kurdish soldier. I turned around to defend myself and came face to face with my commanding officer, ordering me to keep moving. I complained to him about the abuse, but he charged me with disorderly conduct and ordered the low-ranking officer to put me in solitary confinement, which was a tent pitched outside in ninety-degree Fahrenheit heat.

Risking being court-martialed in the war zone for disregarding the chain of command, since I worked with upper echelon military commanders, I disobeyed my commanding officer and went to work. I typed my complaint against my commanding officer for abuse and handed it to the general. While the general was reading my complaint, my commanding officer was descending down the stairs, yelling my name, ordering me to go to solitary confinement. When he saw the general sitting, he froze, and the general asked him to have a seat. He was interrogated by the general and released, and I was told to carry on with my work. I was angry and wanted revenge. On my lunch break, I went to the soldier who slapped me and told him, either he tells the general who put him up to slap me or I will kill him that night, and he better write his goodbye letter to his mother.

It did not take very long time for that soldier, by the help of his officer in charge of military supplies, to confess to being ordered by the lieutenant general to slap me from behind for not being Kurd enough to stay away from other nationalities. By two o'clock in the afternoon, the general gave me a letter to deliver it to my commanding officer. When I gave him the letter, he gave me an angry look, and by four o'clock, the abusing officer had to leave our unit and report to the frontline battalion to start disarming land mines and ammunitions.

I had access to the news at the base about abuses, bribes, and discriminations, and reported them anonymously to the base commanding general, and in a short time, many of the abusers were relocated, demoted, or dishonorably discharged. They had suspected me as the one behind exposing their shenanigans, and at one point, I heard rumors that they had planned to kill me, but the Lord had a different plan for me. I was exposed to anthrax and was taken away to the hospital before they got to me.

Iran was no longer a major oil-producing country, and the consequence of income reduction and loss of foreign currency earning had brought the country onto its knees. Our military machine was crippled. Our jet fighters could not fly to penetrate behind the enemy line. We were relying on our foot soldiers carrying Russian, lousy AK-47 close-combat rifles to win the war against Saddam Hussein, who had the financial support of Saudi Arabia and Kuwait, and the tactical support of the United States and the Soviet Union.

By the United States' permission, Saudi Arabia had leased the AWACS (Airborne warning and control system) spy airplane to Saddam Hussein, and the Iranian army could not make a move without Saddam Hussein's knowledge. We were buying American-made military supplies at the black market value through Germany during President Reagan's administration.

Iran lost between 1–1.5 million military personnel and close to one million maimed soldiers aside from billions of dollars of property damage. The loss of personnel was so rapid that we could not get to the dead bodies on time, and the hungry dogs were feeding on the corps. The heavy stench of the dead bodies in the hundred-degree Fahrenheit summer heat had caused many other diseases that the Iranian army was not equipped to deal with. During the night, not only did we have to guard against Iraqi attacks but also against flesh-eating dogs. We could not shoot the dogs because of shortage of ammunition, but we devised a wooden bat with long nail spikes at the end of the bat to fight the dogs.

Iran used to have heavy mine-clearing tanks with huge spikes in the front made by the United States of America to disarm the land mines in a faster and safer manner, but it was destroyed by Saddam's army, and we were relying on our sappers to do the manual land mine disarming, and most of the time, they ended up losing their arms, legs, and more.

Chapter Eight

War Stories

Land Mines and the Dopeheads

One day, as our unit tried to clear the road, we came across a mine field with mixed pattern land mines, and it was not easy to disarm in a short time. The Islamic army, a totally disorganized militia group (Pasdaran), wanted to move forward, and the mine field had to be cleared. So, in their wisdom, their commander had gone to the village nearby and brought some donkeys so they would run over land mines to clear the field. Sure enough, the first donkey had stepped on the land mine and was blown into pieces. The rest of the donkeys looked at each other, made an about face, and ran the other direction,, and it was said that **the donkeys had more common sense than the dopehead Islamic army.**

But it was not over; they had a plan B. The commander had gone to a village primary school and asked the children eight to ten years old to participate. My officer said that the children came with a headband, saying, "There is no God but Allah, and Mohammad is his messenger," a small Quran in their shirt pocket, a small candle and key, and chanting Allah O Akbar, they ran over the land mines and cleared the way to victory, and they were all torn into pieces. The Quran was their ID as a Muslim, a candle to light their way to heaven, and a key to open heaven's door to enter to receive their rewards.

Saddam Hussein had underestimated his enemy of 60,000,000 numb skulls who were willing to die for the sake of Allah but to give in, versus his 17,000,000 people who ran away or surrendered when push came to shove. Saddam Hussein's army were relying on the United States and Russian support and the backing of Arab countries who were in competition for the control of oil prices in the Persian Gulf.

We were eight comrades in one bunker from different ethnicities: Turks, Kurds and Persians. To be honest, my two years of military service was the best time of my life because no matter how hard we worked, it was a much better life than the one I had back home. We worked hard in the heat, dust, bombardments, thirst, hunger, and sickness, but we were united and happy in spite of it all. At night, we would make tea and gather around and tell stories, jokes, drink tea, and eat local watermelon from nearby villages.

The tea-making soldier

The Tea Thief and Smoke Bomb

One day, we received our cubed sugar and tea rations along with hygiene supplies and uniforms. Two days later, we noticed that our cubed sugar and tea was almost gone. It was supposed to last a month. We asked each other about it, but nobody had an answer to the disappearance of the supplies. One of our comrades was the tea boy for the military officers, and he had access to the bunker during the day while we were busy working in the field. I questioned him about the tea and cubed sugar, and he denied it. When he was out working, I told my other comrades not to drink any tea until I found the tea thief. They asked about my investigation method, but I did not tell them anything. I knew the tea boy had stolen the tea, cubed sugar and drank the rest of it on his break and he would continue to do so.

I went to the field, collected carpenter ants, cut them into small pieces, added some cork pieces, and mixed them with the tea. Ants contain formic acid and when it is mixed with tea, bottle cork, boiled, and consumed by somebody, it will create an excessive amount of gas in the belly and irritate the stomach.

My comrade had come into the bunker on his break, brewed the contaminated tea, and drank it. It was lunch break, and we lined up to receive our lunch. The tea boy was missing, and we found him sitting in the corner of the underground bunker and did not want to move or speak. I knew what had happened. He was extremely flatulent and could not move or say anything without passing loud and smelly gas. I just pushed him gently and, boy oh boy, he started speaking through a different orifice, gas bombing the whole bunker, and running out shooting smoke bombs behind him. That day, we did not need Saddam Hussein's bombers; we had our own. And I announced, "There is your sugar cube and tea thief."

Later on, when he recovered from his state of flatulency, he admitted to stealing the tea and cubed sugar to take them to his family. We ended up giving all our tea and cubed sugar to him so he could take them home.

Soldier Abuser and Hot Lips

I have been taken advantage of since my childhood, and as a grown-up man in the military, I could not tolerate any abuse. We had a unit secretary who was abusive toward soldiers and would discriminate against certain races. He was half-Kurd and half-Turk, and he chose to mix with Kurds more than the Turks. We had worked at the archive office back at the base. I asked him to take it easy on the soldiers, but he boldly said, "What are you going to do about it, if I don't?" I said, "You will find out."

My Christian friend who was the general's driver was on his way to town, and I asked him to get me four pieces of habanero pepper and a pair of rubber gloves. It was summer, and we all slept out in the open under a mosquito net. I wore the rubber gloves, cut the habanero peppers in halves, and rubbed them on my fingers. At midnight, I crawled on my belly toward the unit secretary's bed, opened his mosquito net, rubbed my fingers gently on his cheeks and lips, and quickly crawled back into my bed. Five minutes later, we heard somebody screaming, running around the camp, and asking for water. It was the secretary who was on fire.

In the morning, as we lined up for the morning military routine, the secretary showed up with blisters on his cheeks and lips, and I said, "Hello, beautiful." He got the message, and that was the end of the soldiers' abuse by him.

The Shaken Belief

I stayed committed to my Islamic beliefs, participated in the rituals, and followed the standards of Islam as a daily routine. I read the Quran in detail, and one day, I came across a big controversy in chapter 66 (Surat At-Tahrim), where Mohammad, the prophet of Islam, had sex with Marriah Al-Qiptiah (who was not his wife) on his wife Hifsah's bed, and later on, had a son with her by the name Ibrahim who died in infancy. I brought this to the Muslim leader's attention. He told me to be quiet about it and there was no question in Islam. I was brought up Muslim and had high regard for it, but at that moment, I was very curious and wanted to investigate further. I had believed that Islam was the most comprehensive religion, and it would lead me to God.

I intensified in my deep study of the Quran. The more I read, the more questions I had. I came across verses that directed me to read the book of the prophets of old, like Moses, Job, and Abraham, but I had no access to those books. I had knowledge of the Torah, the Jewish book, and Injeel, the Christian book, but we were told that those books had been distorted and were no longer valid.

Underground mosque

Wrong Target

Another day, we were all working outside, repairing electrical wiring, and right before lunch, an Iraqi MiG 23 appeared in the sky, targeting the southern command center across the field. Their antiaircraft machine gun started shooting, and the Iraqi MiG ended up dropping its bomb on our camp. We ran into the underground shelter for protection, but our eyes went dark, ears hurting and our bellies aching. While in the bunker, one of my comrades fainted, but by the grace of God, I woke him up by slapping and kicking him, and he came back to life and was very grateful. We lost one of our communication vehicles, and one of our sergeants got injured and lost his hearing.

Iraqi bomb shrapnel after explosion with the trigger in my hand

Flash Flood

Two days after the bombing, we had a flash flood. About eight o'clock in the morning as I was heading to work, I saw the dark clouds and asked my comrades to close the opening in the wall we had for ventilation, to keep the rain water out. They ignored my suggestion and we had a flash flood by 10 a.m. By the time I came for lunch, our bunker had three feet of water in it. We had to take all our personal belongings out, dry it, and redirect the rain water from around the bunker.

Redirecting flood water away from the bunker

Missed by a Fraction of an Inch

The Iraqi air force was supported by the Soviet Union and fully operational, and they attacked us daily. One day after lunch, we were trying to take it easy and, suddenly, two Iraqi MiG 23s appeared in the sky; they had dropped their big bombs over the central war command across the field from us, and they all had small rockets and fifty-caliber wing-mounted guns. I was with my Christian friend whom I had met at the base, and the Iraqi jet started firing at us. At first, we thought they were passing by until we heard bullets pass by our ears. My friend, being a city boy, thought that it was the birds flying past his ear, and I forced his head down. At the same time, I felt something scrape my ear. I saw the dust boiling, and it was a hot fifty-caliber bullet that scraped my ear and missed me by a fraction of an inch, and **the Lord was there again to save my life.**

An Unforgettable Friend and a Wounded Heart

As the war intensified and we were losing control of the battle, I kept in touch with my friend who was fifty miles away from me at the front line of the war, and we coordinated our military break to see each other at home for the Persian new year celebration. His arrival was a day ahead of me. I went home to see my grandparents and also visited my friend's parents, expecting to see my friend, but to my surprise, he was late. Two days passed, and early morning, I heard a knock on the door. It was another comrade from his unit who was my friend's classmate too. Seeing him at my front door, I was shocked, and he said that my friend was in the hospital. I asked him, "Dead or alive?" He did not answer the question but wept bitterly. My friend was deployed to the front line. They were settling down and as he was putting the generator together, Iraqis had shelled them from ground and air, and the bomb shells had taken the back of his head and right leg, and he had died.

The Iraqi army was supported by American AWACS (Airborne Warning And Control System) spy airplane, leased to Iraq from Saudi Arabia that provided the Iraqis with my friend's unit's geographical location, and the Iraqis had shelled my friend's unit as they were arriving.

I spent the rest of my vacation at his parents' house attending his long funeral. It was hard to look at his parents' face that even though I had tried my best to keep their son on an easy assignment for eighteen months, I could not save his life. And I remembered my friend's words on the way to the boot camp that he said "I will not make it home alive." How he knew it, is mystery to me.

The Wicked Quicksand

Another classmate who was interested in Islamic studies joined the Islamic seminary and graduated as an Islamic teacher. He wanted to encourage the Islamic army in their fight against Saddam Hussein, crossing over the city of Karbala (Nineveh in the Old Testament), going through Syria, and capturing the city of Jerusalem. He joined the Islamic army and was deployed to Majnoon Islands in the southern war zone. Majnoon Islands were full of quicksand pools.

The Shiite Muslims believe that their twelfth Imam, Imam Mahdi, will appear in the last day and lead them to heaven. The Muslim leaders used that belief to encourage the Muslim soldier in the battle so they would dress in white clothing, ride on a white horse with a sword in their hands, stand in the short distance, and shout "Allah O Akbar," telling the soldiers to carry on the fight against the enemy.

My friend had dressed up in white and had gone out a short distance from the camp with a sword in his hand to perform his duty to encourage his comrades, but he was not familiar with the Majnoon Islands. He had walked on quicksand and drowned. His body was never discovered, and he was considered an Islamic martyr.

Chapter Nine

The Weapons of Mass Destruction

I t was November 1985, a somewhat calm day, and nothing much was happening in the office underground. We had received a new generator, and our unit had added new bunkers and an electrician needed to run new wiring for lights into the bunkers.

The commanding general asked me if I knew anything about electrical wiring, and I said, "Yes, General," then he sent me to help. As we were pulling wires, an Iraqi jet appeared in a distance just about four or five miles away and dropped a bomb, but strangely, it exploded in the air and was like black smoke. We had an idea that it may be a chemical bomb, but there was no warning, and no action was taken, plus even if we had warning, we did not have **masks or atropine** available for use. Due to the discontinued relationship with USA (Iranian previous military supplier), there was a huge shortage of masks and atropine, and the few we had were expired.

It was a mild, windy day. It did not take long for my eyes to go dark, and the last thing I heard was, "Take him to the hospital."

Some time had passed, and I felt that I was in a bed, but it was different and very peaceful. I lifted my head up and noticed that I was in a very big bunker where I could not see the end of it, with so many others sleeping, and everybody was under white sheets and soft white light, and nobody was moving. I thought I was in my bunker and my comrades had forgotten to wake me up for my post. I laid my head down and went back to sleep. A few minutes had passed, and I felt cold. Thinking that my blanket had fallen off me, I tried to reach out for my blanket, but I was not making any progress, and I did not know what to do. I could hear some faint noises, felt a touch on my shoulder, my feet were dragging on some hard floor, and I was laid on some kind of semi-hard flat space.

One day, I opened my eyes and noticed that I was hooked up to two IVs (intravenous), and someone said, "Welcome back, my son." I could not respond. My mouth was dry, and my tongue was glued to the roof of my mouth. I struggled, and he said, "Don't worry, and take it easy; you are alive. You will be OK."

I had no recollection of time. One day, two soldiers lifted me up so I could walk, and I fell on my face. They put me back on the bed and gave me some soup to drink, but I could not hold the food down. By then, I had figured out that I was in the army underground hospital, but I did not know why.

It was a sunny day, two soldiers walked me to the side of the road and put me on the back of a Toyota pickup going toward my military unit. The driver, who I did not know, dropped me at the gate of my unit. Two of my friends helped me into our bunker.

I vaguely remember going to work, and the general asked me about the remaining of my service, but I don't remember the answer I gave.

I don't remember the date, but it was a sunny and mild day, and I had my suitcases, one on each hand, saying goodbye to my comrades and crying.

I remember entering through Grandfather's gate. They **slaughtered a sheep as a thanksgiving to Allah** for my safe return, and I remember the blood on the ground.

One day, I found myself cutting grass in my grandfather's vineyard a distance of 500 miles away from the war zone in Khuzestan where I remembered a bomb exploded. I did not know how I got there. So, I came home, and I greeted Grandfather, and he said, "Oh, my son, you can talk!" I replied, "Of course, I can talk. What do you mean?" He said, "Son, you have not talked much for a long time." I asked him, "How long?" He said, "Almost one year," and he continued that I had come home from the military and had been doing my chores and studies, but I had not talked more than a few words, and he showed me my suitcases.

I opened my suitcases, and on top of it, I found a **Persian New Testament called Injeel** and a note inside it, saying, "When you come to your senses, please go to the military base and get your discharge papers."

The following day, I traveled to my military base and found my commanding officer. He was surprised to see me and said "Oh, Jamshid, you are alive!" I was taken back and asked, "What do mean?" He said, "We have you as MIA" (missing in action), and he asked my whereabouts for one year.

After I told him what I knew, which was not much, he showed me the archived story that I had been exposed to a chemical gas.

After my exposure to anthrax gas, they had transferred me to a war zone underground hospital; there, I was pronounced dead and sent to the morgue. No one knows for sure whether I was dead or in a coma. After a while, they had noticed, I was moving. The morgue attendees had dragged me out, and the doctors had revived me back to life by hydration and penicillin treatment for two months. They had released me from the hospital in early January 1986.

The smoke bomb in the air deployed by Iraqi jet fighters was an **inhalation anthrax,** which causes fever and chills, chest discomfort, shortness of breath, confusion, dizziness, cough, headache, extreme tiredness, body aches, and severe sweats, often drenching, which results in dehydration.

It had taken another year for me to come to my senses. I do not recall much of the fourteen months of my life, just bits and pieces. According to my grandfather, I had been doing most of my physical chores, but my communication had been reduced to a word or two.

I received my discharge papers from the military and went back home. I was not 100 percent yet but more functional.

While I was in the military, I had created a photo album. Looking at the photos helped me regain some of my memories and connect some dots.

Chapter Ten

The Voice

Now the time had come for me to continue my dream of becoming a doctor. Four years had passed since my last attempt to further my study. Education was no longer free in Iran. Uncle had more children and he no longer cared for me. After all, I was an independent thinker and would no longer act as his slave. I had a feeling that my family did not like the idea of me coming back alive. They would have gained more from my dead body than a living one because I would have been a martyr, and my family would have reaped the benefits of martyrdom from the Islamic government, which was financial and a government position.

I went to Grandfather and asked for financial aid for my studies, and he said that they had money, but I did not have any part in it because he had disowned me when I was a child to protect the family inheritance from my mother in case of my death. I said, "Grandpa, I am back alive and am twenty-five years old." He replied that he would make me his son before his death, and I asked, "When are you going to die?" He was shocked and yelled at me, saying, "Do you want me to die?" I said, "Grandpa, it looks like that is the only way I will receive an inheritance from you. He said, "Go to your uncle; he will take care of you."

I asked Uncle for help, and he said that I had no inheritance in the family and unless Grandfather legally made me his son, I would not receive anything. I was shocked and responded to him, saying, "So, you lied to me when you said you are my brother when I was four years old." He said, "That is an old story; get a life. Do whatever you like," and add to that, his wife had told my auntie that if I claimed any inheritance, she would shed blood in the family.

I pondered for a minute and did some fast calculation. According to Islamic law, Grandfather can disown his children in any way he wishes, and I had no recourse, and the only way I could have an inheritance would be if Uncle was no more.

I did not know what to do or where to take my case. We had a Muslim neighbor whose son was shot dead in a crossfire between the Kurdish freedom fighters and Islamic army while working on the farm. Our neighborhood was a war zone, and he did not have a case against the government. One day, we were driving home from the farm and saw our neighbor hitchhiking home, and my uncle gave him a ride in his car. We asked him about his case against the government, and he said that he could not do anything about it but had taken his case to God himself and had given God ten days to answer him back. My uncle thought that he had gone mad.

A week had passed, and we saw him again and gave him a ride home. My uncle asked him about his son and family. He said that God had answered his plea. The man who had shot his son was himself shot dead not too far from the place that he shot his son, and he was praising God, saying, "God is alive and well."

Uncle was part of an anti-Islamic, pro-Shah organization, and I knew where they had their meetings. I was part of an Islamic training group, if I somehow would have my uncle arrested and killed, I would have whatever I wanted, but I wanted to do it legally.

I told my uncle that I would see him in my court. He was taken back and slowly moved away. I was angry and felt betrayed, so I isolated myself from the family and stayed in the barn.

First things first, I decided to follow our neighbor's path and take my case to God, and I gave God seven days to answer my plea. My uncle's wife was pregnant with a son. It was time to take her to the hospital for delivery. He took his wife to a private hospital. Six days later, she gave birth to a healthy boy. Everybody was happy, and there was a huge celebration over the second male baby in the family.

On the seventh day, my uncle went to bring his wife and the baby home from the hospital. Upon his arrival to the hospital, he had found out that the baby had died just hours earlier.

He sued the hospital for mishandling the baby. The court ordered an autopsy but to everybody's surprise they found no reason for the baby's death. The case was closed and Uncle and his wife came home empty-handed.

Uncle and his wife were heartbroken. His wife looked me in the eyes and asked me a question with a stern voice, saying, "What have you done? Have you taken your case to God?" And I said, "Yes, I have, but your problem is not with me; you may take your case to him too. After all, He is the ultimate judge." She went quietly and wept bitterly.

Empty handed and with no savings account with a little money from my military days, I started to look for a job in a war-torn country. I talked to friends and old classmates and found a twelve-hour shift job as a chemical technician in the sugar factory ten miles away from my hometown. I worked twelve-hour night shifts and twelve-hour day shifts for thirty dollars a month. I used my high school bicycle to travel back and forth to work.

One night on my fifteen-minute break, I noticed flashing of lights in the sky. From my experience in the war, I gathered it was Iraqi jets taking photos of industrial zones preparing for attack the next day. I notified my head engineer and coworkers of the coming disaster and told them to evacuate the area the next day. Sure enough, by 11 a.m. the next day, Iraqi MiGs appeared in the sky and bombed the factory, sugar silos, residential facilities next to the factory, and I lost the only job I had.

I went back to check after the bombing, and I saw body parts, blood on the street, and an out-of-order factory. Many of us could not go back to work in the factory, even after it was operational because it was an Iraqi target.

Desperate for work, I talked to my friends and my brother in-law who was a member of the Islamic army about becoming a Muslim judge. They directed me, and I started the process. I passed the physical exam, criminal background check, and I started to study for preliminary Sharia law test.

As I was gathering my religious books to study, I came across the New Testament that my Christian friend had left in my suitcase. I studied the New Testament, so one day, I could reason with my friend and invite him to Islam. As I read the New Testament, I decided to write my reasoning that the Christians had changed the Bible and the Bible was corrupt.

The day came, and I sat for my religious test and passed. I came home and packed my suitcase so I could leave the family for good to be trained for a judicial position.

I went to Grandfather, kissed his hand, and said, "Grandpa, even though you have left me empty-handed and homeless, I thank you for teaching me how to be a man. I have chosen to forgive you, but as for me and my uncle, I will set him straight." He asked, "What are you going to do with him?" I said, "You will hear it; it will be loud." **What I meant by that was to execute my uncle for being anti-Islamic Republic, marry his wife, raise his children, perform my Islamic duty to my deceased uncle, and get my inheritance back.**

Heavy-hearted, I came back to the barn, picked up my suitcases, and started moving. Before I got to the exit door, I heard a voice calling, "**Come to me.**" I turned around and did not see anyone. I thought I was hallucinating. I ignored the voice, but I heard it for the second time, saying, "**Come to me.**" This time, my knees shook, and I was on the ground, weeping. I had no idea why I was weeping. After a while, I got myself together and started to process the three words, and I remembered that I had seen those words somewhere. Desperate for an answer, I opened my suitcase, and the last book I had read was the Bible. I kept flipping the pages until I came to **Matthew 11:28-30 NIV,** where Jesus says: "**Come to me**, all you who are weary and burdened, and I will give you rest. Take my yoke upon you and learn from me, for I am gentle and humble in heart, and you will find rest for your souls. For my yoke is easy and my burden is light," and this portion of the scripture was titled in Farsi with three words: **Come to me.**

I was perplexed and did not understand; how could the words of a book communicate to a person? We used to read the Quran and memorize it; most Muslims do not understand, and even those who do understand the meaning of the Quran never claim that the words of the Quran can talk to them.

My analysis of the situation was that I read the Bible and was demon-possessed. That idea came from the Quran that demons could talk to a person as they talked to Mohammad, the prophet of Islam.

April 15, 1987, not knowing how to get rid of the demons, in my desperation, I called my Christian friend who had left the Bible in my suitcase and told him the story. He replied that they were not demons, but God was calling me because he had been praying for my salvation. I could not wrap my mind around it because, for the Muslims, God was far away and does not communicate to anyone except the prophets. We all are sinners except chosen prophets who are holy; never mind the sins of the prophets, which are mentioned in their books.

As I explained to him the rest of my life story, he invited me to his house. He lived in the southwest region, which was still the war zone at that time, and I lived in the northwest corner of the country. I accepted his invitation for two reasons: 1. I no longer had a home, and 2. I was trying to get rid of the demons that had possessed me by reading his book, and I thought maybe he would have a way to get the demons out of me.

Chapter Eleven

A New Birth

O n April 16, 1987, I picked up my suitcases, purchased a bus ticket, and went to see him. We had a lot to talk about, and we discussed the demons, but he showed me from the Bible that it was truly God who was calling me. First, I thought, he was trying to make me a Christian, and I resisted and tried to convince him to become a Muslim because I believed that Islam was the last religion! At the end of our discussion, he offered to pray for me. I had nothing against prayer; after all, we Muslims prayed five times a day and made fun of Christians who prayed less than we did.

Not knowing the custom, I asked him the direction to which we were going to pray; he said that God was everywhere. "We Christians bow our head and close our eyes and pray." He said, "Let's close our eyes." I did not trust him. I kept one eye open just to make sure he would not make me a Christian.

He started saying, "Heavenly Father, I come before You as a sinner, and I repent of my sins. Please forgive my sins. Thank You for Your grace and forgiveness through Jesus Christ" (I was ok with that), and he continued, "Thank You for giving Your Son who died on the cross for my sins and rose again from the dead (I was not ok with that but agreed halfway because there is more than one place in the Quran testifying to the fact that Jesus was born, died, and resurrected from the dead, but there is only one place that the Quran mentions Jesus was not crucified but it appeared to the Jew that He was), and he continued, "I believe in Jesus Christ as my Lord and Savior," and he finished his prayer with the word **amen.**

The word **amen** caught my attention as though it connected with my spirit because Muslims pray the first chapter of the Quran seventeen times a day and always finish it with the word **amen.** No one in Islam knows the reason for the existence of the word amen in the Quran, but it is there. Some believe that the first chapter of the Quran is a pre-Islamic prayer that Othman the third Kaliph put in the Quran. This chapter has nothing to do with Islam. It is a generic prayer that anybody can pray to their god. But when I said amen this time, it had a different meaning, as though I was accepting something real that I never meant before. **I accepted Christ as my Savior and King.**

I opened my second eye, and I was not the same. I thought I was drunk and went to sleep. When I woke up in the morning of April 18, 1987, everything was different and new. I asked my friend about it, and he said that **I had been born again,** according to John 3:3, where Jesus says: "Very truly I tell you, no one can see the kingdom of God unless they are born again."

I had read the New Testament, and I knew the stories of the Bible. I had written against it with proof from the Quran and Islamic books that Christians had changed the Bible, but when my friend explained the fatherhood of God through Christ and the forgiveness of the sins provided by His sacrifice on the cross, it made sense that the penalty of my sins were paid for, and I was free.

I believed him because my friend had displayed a Christlike life throughout our friendship in the military. I knew him as an honest and loving friend who had dared to leave a New Testament in my suitcase when he had helped me go home after my exposure to anthrax. He was Jesus in the flesh to me. He was the Bible that I had not read and the walking/talking Jesus that I had not met before.

And he said that **I am a child of God,** according to John 1:12.

He came to that which was his own, but his own did not receive him. Yet to all who did receive him, to those who believed in his name, he gave the right to become children of God— children born not of natural descent, nor of human decision or a husband's will, but born of God. (John 1:11-13 NIV).

My feelings had changed, and I no longer hated my uncle, and I lost my desire to have him killed. The first thing that came to my mind was to forgive him. I took a piece of paper and wrote on it: "Uncle, I have embraced Christ Jesus. My life has changed. I do not need my inheritance; I forgive you, and I will not kill you," and I mailed it to him.

Suddenly, I felt a big load was lifted off my shoulders as though some heavy load was holding me down, and I felt so light that I could fly and realized that **my healing began with forgiveness.**

I no longer felt depressed, angry, abused, or sad, but I had confidence that the Creator of heaven and earth had become my Father, and I could call Him my Father in heaven. Even though I did not know what tomorrow held, but I knew Jesus held my tomorrow.

I did not change my religion, but I received the right which I did not deserve through Christ to become a child of God. *I was a new man.*

I no longer had any use for any religion, no matter the name, but I received a relationship with God Himself through His Son, who paid the penalty of my sins and reconciled me with the Father, and I was adopted to God's family through His Son Jesus Christ, and God had become a father to a fatherless like me.

Islam, at its best, was a religion. It commands repentance and seeking forgiveness, but never guarantees forgiveness because the penalty of sin has not been paid; therefore, there is no reconciliation between God and man. And all there is, is a hope based upon man's good behavior, which amounts to nothingness.

In Islam, Muslims die for Allah to receive high points to enter heaven, but in Christ, God became flesh, humbled Himself, and became a man to die for mankind's sin to pay the penalty of their sins and bring mankind home to heaven.

As a Shiite Muslim, I bemoaned the horrific death of Imam Hossein, the grandchild of Mohammad, the prophet of Islam, and beat my chest and cried one month every year to gain points toward entering heaven, but as a born-again child of God, I did not need to gain points toward heaven because I was counted righteous based on the righteousness of Christ Jesus.

Christ was born of a Jewish woman who was conceived by the Holy Spirit who came from the Father; therefore, God Himself is the Father of Jesus Christ.

Jesus Christ was not a Christian, and I was not converted by anyone to Christianity; rather, I was reconciled with God the Father through Christ Jesus, who paid the penalty of my sins, died on the cross, and rose again from the dead on the third day, and I was justified by faith through Christ and counted innocent based on what Jesus did on my behalf. Therefore, when God the Creator looks at me on judgment day, He looks at me through His Son and His righteousness. I am a Christian because I believe in Christ as my Lord and Savior, I do not believe in Christianity as my new religion, but I have a personal relationship with God Himself through Christ Jesus, His Son.

Throughout my life, I had suffered abuse, humiliation, and had many wounds and scars, but as I read the Bible, I found that Christ is preparing a home in heaven for me, and ***the only one with scars in heaven will be Christ Himself***, as we read in Revelation 21:1–5:

> Then I saw a new heaven and a new earth, for the first heaven and the first earth had passed away, and the sea was no more. And I saw the holy city, new Jerusalem, coming down out of heaven from God, prepared as a bride adorned for her husband. And I heard a loud voice from the throne saying, "Behold, the dwelling place of God is with man. He will dwell with them, and they will be his people, and God himself will be with them as their God. He will wipe away every tear from their eyes, and death shall be no more, neither shall there be mourning, nor crying, nor pain anymore, for the former things have passed away.

As a Muslim, I was a mess, but in Christ, I became a message of hope to those who are seeking it with all their hearts.

I was a Muslim all of my life, and I always pondered on the verses of the Quran and questioned it, but the ignorant teachers of Islam would say, "There is no question in the Quran," and shut me up, and at best, they would refer me to the book of Jonah in Quran chapter ten, verse 94: "So, if you are in doubt concerning that which We have revealed unto you, then ask those who are reading the Book before you. Verily, the truth has come to you from your Lord. So be not of those who doubt (it)."

So, the Quran refers Muslims to ask the people of the book, **the Jews and Christians,** about what the Muslims do not understand in the Quran.

When Muslims say that Jesus did not die, we need to respectfully ask for an explanation of the following verse in Surat Al-Imran verse 55: "And (remember) when Allah said: "O `Isa! (Jesus) I will take you and raise you to Myself and purify (save) you from those who disbelieve, and I will make those who follow you superior to those who disbelieve till the Day of Resurrection. Then you will return to Me and I will judge between you in the matters in which you used to dispute."

Clearly, their god says that he will take Jesus to himself, meaning he will kill Him and then raise Jesus to Himself, meaning resurrect Him from the dead. According to this verse, God Himself makes people who believe in Jesus, superior to those who do not believe in Jesus, including Muslims. This makes Muslims infidels.

The question is, why did God take Jesus to Himself (kill Him) and raise Him from the dead?

The answer is found in the book of the people, the Bible, that mankind could not pay the penalty of their sins through their works, but God, in His mercy, laid the penalty of our sins on His Son, who was and is holy and able to suffer for our sins, satisfy the judge, and raise Him from the dead, so we can be free from sin and guilt and enter God's presence.

In the chapter of Mary, verse 15, we read in the Quran about John the Baptist:

"(peace) be on him the day he was born, and the day he dies, and the day he will be raised up to life again."

The Quran testifies about John the Baptist's miraculous birth, death, and resurrection.

Jesus, in Matthew 17:12–13, says: "'**But I tell you that Elijah has already come, and they did not recognize him, but did to him whatever they pleased. So also, the Son of Man will certainly suffer at their hands.' Then the disciples understood that he was speaking to them of John the Baptist.**"

And again, in the chapter of Mary, verse 33, Jesus says about Himself: "(peace) be upon me the day I was born, and the day I die, and the day I shall be raised alive!)"

Here is Jesus testifying about His birth, death, and resurrection, which is the gospel. I wonder where Mohammad got theses verses from? Did I say plagiarism? Yes, of course he did. The Quran was revealed to Mohammad, but it was not by Yahweh, the only God, but someone else, and it was totally plagiarized from different sources. This explains why there is no continuity in the story of Quran. There is no beginning and no end. It is a compilation of many stories from many different religious books.

Chapter Twelve

The Potter and the Clay

I was raised a farmer and learned about seed sowing, vine dressing, sheep herding, and we had boat makers and potters in our neighborhood, and these skills helped me understand the gospel better.

I had read the New Testament several times and had noticed Jesus questioning the questioner, and trying to understand the change in my life, I asked a simple question of Jesus. **How is this possible that a hateful heart can change to a loving and forgiving heart?**

Jesus, in His grace, in a vision, took me to a potter's house. There in the potter's house, I saw the red dirt piled up and covered to keep it moist; next to it, there were fine gravels, circling around. I saw the potter behind the wheel and the clay on top of it. Next to it, there were pots made and left to dry, then I saw the fiery furnace with pots inside being cooked. To the side of the furnace, there was a big barrel of water, and the last, there were pots ready to be shipped to the market.

I heard a voice in my spirit, saying:

Do you see the red dirt? That is you. I picked you up from the field where you were trampled on and abused; the gravels are your sins and transgressions that I removed from you. I am the Potter, and the clay on the wheel is you. I am shaping and forming you according to My will. The pot that is left to dry is you. I took your father and your mother, your inheritance, your home, and all you had from you; you have nobody but Me. I am not done yet. You see the furnace; you are going in to be tried in the fire, and after that, you will be tested in the water. Once you come out in one piece, I will pour My spirit in you, then you will be my vessel of honor and a witness to My name for My glory.

I was humbled, and it was clear that I was saved from my past, and God Himself held my life in His hands, as clay in the potters hands.

The gravels in the clay are usually limestones or softer materials, and they should be removed. The redness in the dirt is iron that gives the dirt strength and its red color. Once the cooking process is over, the potter dips the pot in the water, and limestone, which now is turned to lime, will dissolve and create a hole in the pot, and that pot will be thrown away because it will not hold water.

In the same manner, if our sins are not confessed before the Lord and forgiven through the precious blood of His Son, they will be a hinderance, and Jesus will have no use for us. Because God's holiness and our sins are like water and oil respectively, and they don't mix with each other. No matter how we try to mix our sins, which is like oil, and God's holiness, which is like water, using religion, our good deeds or any other ways to manipulate, our sins always end up on the surface and show their ugly face. God cannot tolerate sin.

The word of the Lord, in Psalm 103:12 AMP, sa**ys: "As far as the east is from the west, So far has He removed our transgressions from us."**

They call me a convert, but I call myself transformed. Yes, I was transformed from the darkness of Islam to the light, who is Jesus, as He said in John 8:12, "**Again, Jesus spoke to them, saying, 'I am the light of the world. Whoever follows me will not walk in darkness, but will have the light of life.'**"

As the **sun**light is the best disinfectant for the germs, so is the blood of Jesus, the **Son** of God is the best disinfectant for sin.

Again, we read in Ephesians 5:8–14:

> **For at one time you were darkness, but now you are light in the Lord. Walk as children of light (for the fruit of light is found in all that is good and right and true), and try to discern what is pleasing to the Lord. Take no part in the unfruitful works of darkness, but instead expose them. For it is shameful even to speak of the things that they do in secret. But when anything is exposed by the light, it becomes visible, for anything that becomes visible is light. Therefore, it says, "Awake, O sleeper, and arise from the dead, and Christ will shine on you."**

As a Muslim, I used to pray to Allah to lead me to the straight path seventeen times a day.

Since Muslims pray to be led in a straight path, they acknowledge that they are walking in a path that is not straight (the path of Satan), but so far, Muslims have not found the straight path. The path that Muslims are looking for is the one that leads to God Himself, but truly, who and where is the straight path? Islam says if we can't find the answer in the Quran, we should ask the people of the books before Islam.

So, I searched the Christian book, and I found in the book of John 14:1–6:

> **Let not your hearts be troubled. Believe in God; believe also in me. In my Father's house are many rooms. If it were not so, would I have told you that I go to prepare a place for you? And if I go and prepare a place for you, I will come again and will take you to myself, that where I am you may be also. And you know the way to where I am going." Thomas said to him, "Lord, we do not know where you are going. How can we know the way?" Jesus said to him, "I am the way, and the truth, and the life. No one comes to the Father except through me.**

I am no longer lost because Jesus promised to be with me and guide me. He said in John 14:15–18:

> **If you love me, keep my commandments. And I will ask the Father, and he will give you**

another Helper, to be with you forever, even the Spirit of truth, whom the world cannot receive, because it neither sees him nor knows him. You know him, for he dwells with you and will be in you. I will not leave you as orphans, I will come to you.

I call the Holy spirit my GPS (**G**od **P**ositioning **S**ystem), who guides me inside-out so I don't have to ask for the way because the way is in me.

I heard someone say that the **Bible** stands for **B**asic **I**nstructions **B**efore **L**eaving **E**arth. So as the owner of a heating and air conditioning company, I always tell my employees, if everything fails, please read the instructions.

The world is in turmoil, spinning out of control, confusion is rampant, man tries to fix it, and everybody has a different idea. Different religions and ideologies claim to have the solution, and they are competing with each other, fighting over, and killing each other, but their ideas are as imperfect and inadequate as they themselves and doomed to fail and are failing. So why not **read the instruction, the Bible,** that came from the Maker of this world, and get it right, but the arrogant spirit that comes from the prince of this world, Satan, prevents them from doing so.

The world is a dark place and is ruled by the prince of the darkness, and for me, it was darker as a Muslim, and I needed a light to walk through this dark place. **Islam did not and could not offer that light,** but I found the light in Jesus as He says in John 8:12, **"I am the light of the world. Whoever follows me will not walk in darkness, but will have the light of life."**

As a Muslim, I had a hard time smiling because in Islam, the more pious you are, the more points you receive toward your good deeds, but as a child of God, I am happy because Jesus has taken away my sorrows and has given me His joy everlasting. We read in Psalm 30:11 NIV, **"You turned my wailing into dancing; you removed my sackcloth and clothed me with joy."**

As a Muslim, I was always disturbed, and there was a battle churning inside me. I was always trying to take revenge. As a member of a twenty-million army against the Jews, we always tried to come up with new ways to kill and destroy the Jews and Christians. One of the ways was how to slit an infidel's throat in less than three seconds, using a knife or hand. But in Christ, I have a peace that surpasses all my understanding. Jesus said in John 14:27 NIV, **"Peace I leave with you; my peace I give you. I do not give to you as the world gives. Do not let your hearts be troubled and do not be afraid."**

As an abused orphan, I was always worried about my next meal, clothing, and shelter, but in Christ, I am confident and have no fear of tomorrow because He cares for me, as He promised in the book of life in Matthew 6:25–34:

> **Therefore, I tell you, do not be anxious about your life, what you will eat or what you will drink, nor about your body, what you will put on. Is not life more than food, and the body more than clothing? Look at the birds of the air: they neither sow nor reap nor gather into barns, and yet your heavenly Father feeds them. Are you not of more value than they? And which of you by being anxious can add a**

single hour to his span of life? And why are you anxious about clothing? Consider the lilies of the field, how they grow: they neither toil nor spin, yet I tell you, even Solomon in all his glory was not arrayed like one of these. But if God so clothes the grass of the field, which today is alive and tomorrow is thrown into the oven, will he not much more clothe you, O you of little faith? Therefore, do not be anxious, saying, "What shall we eat?" or "What shall we drink?" or "What shall we wear?" For the Gentiles seek after all these things, and your heavenly Father knows that you need them all. But seek first the kingdom of God and his righteousness, and all these things will be added to you. Therefore, do not be anxious about tomorrow, for tomorrow will be anxious for itself. Sufficient for the day is its own trouble.

Chapter Thirteen

An Ambassador for Christ

Two days after I gave my life to Christ Jesus, on April 19, 1987, I was hired by the Islamic government as an administrator in a workshop that was in charge of building a military hospital for the Islamic army. I was upfront with the hiring engineer and told him that I was an ex-Muslim. He said it was none of his business who I worshiped. My job was to manage the employees, write contracts, receive incoming trade professionals, and guide them through the project.

The Lord put me in the middle of a fiery furnace, and I was a witness to an entire workshop of workers who were Muslims and leaders of this Islamic organization.

I had threats to my life, but the Lord gave me grace, and I shared the gospel in love. They called me an apostate, but I told them that I was a child of God, and then they would ask me, "How did you become a child of God?" Then I would answer them according to 1 Peter 3:13–17:

> Now who is there to harm you if you are zealous for what is good? But even if you should suffer for righteousness' sake, you will be blessed.

Have no fear of them, nor be troubled, **but in your hearts honor Christ the Lord as holy, always being prepared to make a defense to anyone who asks you for a reason for the hope that is in you; yet do it with gentleness and respect,** having a good conscience, so that, when you are slandered, those who revile your good behavior in Christ may be put to shame. For it is better to suffer for doing good, if that should be God's will, than for doing evil.

The Lord's favor was with me. The Muslims received Bibles from me and also supported our church's physical needs, such as cheese, meat, bread, and butter in the middle of a food shortage in the country. They gave me a place to stay, food to eat, and the salary of an engineer, which I did not deserve. I was in charge of recruiting, and I hired several other ex-Muslims from our church to work on the project.

We read in Psalm 37:25 NIV, "I was young and now I am old, yet I have never seen the righteous forsaken or their children begging bread."

One day as I was busy typing the project contracts, a Muslim leader and his bodyguard came to my office so I would show them the progress.

I read my Bible every day and that day, my Bible was open on my desk, and I was not supposed to read my Bible in the Islamic organization. The Muslim leader, without asking my permission, had turned my Bible around and started reading my Bible, and I was unaware of it. He asked me, "Where did you get that book?" I was startled and realized that he was reading my Bible, and being an ex-military, I kept my composure and said, "I got it from the library, sir." He said, "Which library?" I said, "Church library." He said, "Do you go to church?" I said, "Yes." He continued, "So that makes you a Christian?" And I said, "I am a child of God, and people call me a Christian because I follow Christ as my Lord and Savior." He said, "Can I have this book?" I replied, "Yes, sir," and he offered to pay for it, but I refused to accept money for the Bible. He asked me, "How did you became a child of God?" As I was explaining the father-hood of God in my life, his bodyguard interrupted and told him not to touch the Bible because it was changed, and pointing at me, he said that I was an apostate and should be killed. At this point, I realized that I had a dilemma in my hand, and I started to share my testimony with the bodyguard, but I had to work, and I offered to tell my story in detail if he attended Jesus's birthday party the next day, and it was Christmas. **The Lord was present,** and they both accepted my invitation and came to our Christmas party. I invited all the Muslim engineers and leaders of the project, and we had more Muslims in our church than Christians for Christmas 1988. The bodyguard and Muslim leader showed up, and the bodyguard received a Bible and got his answers.

As a new believer in Christ, I was surrounded by believers who adopted me as their own, discipled me, and helped me in my walk with Christ Jesus. We had regular Bible studies on a weekly basis, and mature believers would invite me to their house for a meal and overnight stay and show me how to live as a Christian.

They became Jesus in the flesh for me and taught me how to love my neighbor as myself. They showed me the power of forgiveness and love of others. They taught me how to love my enemies and pray for them.

I took on responsibilities in the church as gardener, maintenance man, and in the library.

One day, I was working in the office of an Islamic hospital project when the gatekeeper came and told me that a woman was asking for me. I never knew a woman in my life, so I asked him to bring her in. To my surprise, it was my mother and half-brother. I used to live in a project housing area, so I took my mother and half-brother to my friend's house, and the next day, it was Friday. I took my mother and half-brother to church, and they heard the gospel of Jesus Christ. My mother was surrounded by the believers and was surprised by their love and respect for her.

She said, "Son, I don't understand much of what I see, but this is much better than what we believe in Islam. And this was the first time that a parent of an ex-Muslim had entered the church and sat down to hear the gospel in an Iranian church.

She left three days later with confidence that her orphaned son had a Father who cared for him, and he was going to be all right.

Since it was against the law to preach the gospel to Muslims, ex-Muslims would not be baptized in the church after their conversion until they showed maturity in Christ and signed a petition/affidavit requesting to be baptized on their own recourse, so the government could not hold the church responsible for their conversion, and the member would strictly be responsible for making the decision to be baptized. This process usually would take a year or two depending on the believer's growth in Christ.

When I came to church for the first time, I surrendered my specialty knife to the pastor as a sign of total physical surrender to Christ because I did not feel that I had any use for it anymore, but I looked rough and tough, and I heard later that the believers had a hard time trusting me, and they had thought of me as a government spy.

One Friday in September 1987, after a church meeting, my pastor asked me to stay back for a meeting, and I was taken back, thinking I had done something wrong. I was very anxious until I entered the meeting, and to my surprise, I saw all the church leaders sitting around and smiling. I was still not sure what was going to happen until they told me that I was ready to be baptized. On September 21, 1987, I signed the affidavit and got baptized in the small garden pool of two-foot-deep water.

After second round of deep Bible study and passing the written test, I was encouraged to pray and be baptized in the Holy Spirit. I had no clue, but my pastor assured me that once it happened, I would understand. I kept reading Acts 2 and prayed until I was baptized in the Holy Spirit on February 28, 1988.

Since 90 percent of our church members were comprised of ex-Muslims, the government came, arrested our pastor, and banished him to the capital city, and we had a new pastor and were spied on daily by the government office across the street from the church.

Leaving the darkness of Islam and Satan's territory is costly. The prince of darkness comes after those who vacated their position and tries to take them back. As ex-Muslims, we became the target of Satan with a bull's eye on our backs.

The church had appointed me as the keeper of the church at night. One night, as I slept in the upper room of the church, the government authorities tried to break into church to vandalize the building, and I yelled at them, and knowing that there was someone in the church, they left.

The Muslim's mind is Satan's workshop. I was trained to practice Islam from the young age of four, and everything I did was ingrained in me. Hatred was a part of me, killing infidels (non-Muslim) was the practice of the day. Taking revenge was justified, an eye for an eye and a tooth for a tooth (borrowed from Judaism). Love of others applies only to the same Muslim sect, not to anyone else. Peace can only be between Muslims of the same sect or non-Muslims who convert to Islam. Lying and deception are justified as long as it promotes Islamic ideology.

In the summer of 1988, again on Friday after the church meeting, my pastor asked me and a few others to take a week off work and attend a faith-building Bible study. We paid for our food, accommodation and took on a solid daily prayer and Bible study on the foundation of faith through Ezra and Nehemiah.

Following the Bible study, the church sent four of the believers, including me, to a church camp meeting in the capital city in the garden of Sharon for another week of training. We were trained by the leaders of the Iranian Assembly of God church, and the government spies were taking our photos from the walls of the garden, and that was the last Christian camp training we had in Iran. **Our leader told us that very soon he would be arrested and killed, and we should expect the same.**

The Iranian government increased their pressure on the churches all over the country and started arresting the new believers, torturing, bribing, and intimidating them to come back to Islam. Some of the members left the country. Our second pastor was taken to jail, and we were left without a pastor again and were told to make a decision because we were next.

The government officials came to our work places and told us that they knew where we worked, and one day, they would take us to jail. Jesus did not promise us an easy life after being born again, but He said in John 16:31–33:

> Jesus answered them, "Do you now believe? Behold, the hour is coming, indeed it has come, when you will be scattered, each to his own home, and will leave me alone. Yet I am not alone, for the Father is with me. I have said these things to you, that in me you may have peace. In the world you will have tribulation. But take heart; I have overcome the world."

Chapter Fourteen

Life in Exile

I prayed about my situation, and the Lord gave me peace to leave the country, but I did not know where and how.

In Genesis 12:1, we read, "Now the Lord said to Abram, 'Go from your country and your kindred and your father's house to the land that I will show you.'"

I took a week off and went to the capital city, Tehran, to find a way out, but I came back empty-handed. One of my Arab drivers came to my office and asked my whereabouts for the past week, and I told him that I was on a vacation. He looked at me and said, "Are you trying to get out of the country?" I was taken back and thought, "He is a spy." I asked him, "Why do you care? And what can you do about it?" He said that he could get me a visa to the United Arab Emirates. Up until then, I had not given any thought about the UAE, but that was a way out. So, I gave him some money, and he got a visa in a week. I had not traveled abroad before, and I had no idea how to go about it. He told me that I needed an airplane ticket, and I asked, "Where can I get a ticket?" He said he would get the ticket. I gave him the money for the ticket, and he got me the ticket the next day.

The Lord was there, and He made a way when there was no way.

The Lord's Presence before Me

On January 10, 1989, I left Iran and arrived in Dubai the same day. I landed with two boxes of books and Bibles and a suitcase of clothes. The airport officer asked me about the content of the boxes, and I said they were books and Bibles, and he said, "Welcome to Dubai." I laid my boxes and suitcase by the side of the road and waited for a taxi to take me to a hotel. An old man in his late sixties showed up and asked me "Where are you going, son?" I said, "Waiting for taxi to take me to a hotel." He told me to follow him, and he picked up my two boxes of the books that weighed about fifty pounds each and put them on his shoulders, and moved ahead. I was only twenty-seven years old and had a hard time catching up with him. He took me to a hotel, put the boxes down, and told the hotel receptionist that I was his friend and asked them to take good care of me. The hotel charged me only a fraction of the actual cost. I put down my suitcase and turned around to thank the old man, but he was gone. I asked the receptionist about the old man, and he said, "What old man? I told him, "The old man who just talked to you about me." He said that he thought the heat was getting to me and I needed to rest; there was no old man.

It was against the law to bring Bibles to the UAE, but the officer was blinded by the Lord.

I was a stranger in the land, and the Lord's angel was before me to guide me to a safe place.

The Lord spoke to Moses in Exodus 33:12-14:

> Moses said to the Lord, "See, you say to me, 'Bring up this people,' but you have not let me know whom you will send with me. Yet you have said, 'I know you by name, and you have also found favor in my sight.' Now therefore, if I have found favor in your sight, please show me now your ways, that I may know you in order to find favor in your sight. Consider too that this nation is your people." And he said, "My presence will go with you, and I will give you rest."

I knew how to read and write English and Arabic, but I had not spoken those languages. I came across an Iranian who was familiar with Dubai. I purchased an English and Arabic electric type writers and partnered with my newfound friend to fill out visiting visa forms for the immigration office as a subcontractor. We were making good money until somebody broke into our apartment and stole my typewriters.

After three months, my money ran out, and I could not get a job to feed myself. I had no way forward, and I could not go back home. My family had denied me, my church was shut down, and my friends were scattered.

Someone suggested to appeal to the United Nations for refugee status. I went to the United Nations office in Abu Dhabi and applied for asylum but I got rejected due to having a valid passport, and I could not make a case for not being able to go back to Iran. At the same time, I found out that Iranian mercenaries were looking for political and religious asylees to assassinate them.

I had two Kurdish friends with me who had ran away from Iran for fear of joining military. We found an Iraqi Kurdish contractor in a small town called AL-Ain, part of the UAE, who would hire us as construction workers, and we journeyed together to AL-Ain.

Al-Ain is a small town with gushing springs and, compared to other UAE cities, was cooler and greener. It had few small hills with views. Many rich Arabs lived in that city, and because of cooler temperatures, construction of new houses were booming.

There were workers from many different nationalities in the construction field. We worked with Hindus, Afghanis, Arabs from Egypt, Somalia, Syria, Palestine, Yemen, Iraq, Lebanon, and Iranians.

Iranians were not favored in Arabia. Racial discrimination was very rampant. Unless you knew somebody in the construction zone, you could not get any job. Sometimes a big fight would break out between different nationalities, many of whom did not have work permits, and when police would show up, they would flee in different directions.

The city was well organized. There were small local malls in every neighborhood, and the stores were well supplied with good and luxury items from different countries. I did not have enough money to rent a place to stay, so I slept in the building where I worked. The local malls had public bathrooms and running water, and I used to take showers in those bathrooms.

The offices and stores were run by foreign nationals and, if by chance, foreign nationals had to leave the country, the UAE would be totally paralyzed. Arabs were not able to cook, clean, run the government, or defend themselves.

When Saddam Hussein attacked Kuwait, all of the foreign nationals who were members of the UAE defense forces resigned and went back to their home country, and the Arabs had to depend on US forces to defend themselves against Saddam Hussein.

Many male and female workers were hired as domestic workers from India, Bangladesh, Sri Lanka, Philippines, Syria, Lebanon, and Yemen. They were abused physically and sexually and forced to work sixteen to eighteen hours a day. This was and is a different form of slavery. At their arrival, their passports were confiscated, and they could not leave or change employment without permission from their sponsors (slave owners); otherwise, they would be charged with absconding.

Rich Arab sheiks who had numerous wives would spend the nights in fancy hotels with foreign prostitutes, and their wives would sexually abuse their male drivers as sex slaves. This was a big phenomenon as the sheiks would find their children at birth looking like Indians, Filipinos, or other nationalities.

I worked as a pipe fitter for a plumbing company. We worked for a rich sheik who had four wives. The youngest wife was younger than the sheik's daughter from his first wife. He had four drivers and five maids. There were different houses for each wife and corresponding children.

There was a rich sheik whose wife was due to give birth to a boy. After the birth of the child, the sheik had found out that the baby was of Filipino race and questioned his wife about it. She admitted that the baby belonged to the Filipino driver. To cover up his tracks, the sheik divorced his wife and allowed her to marry his Filipino driver, gave him a house in his property, and kept the driver employed as his driver.

He admitted that it was his mistake for not being home for his wife, and the driver and his wife were innocent. These kinds of activities are very common all over Arabia, especially in Saudi Arabia. It was in the news that in Saudi Arabia, an Indian driver was sexually abused by the wives of a rich sheik and died. It was reported that the driver was killed by a camel. There was a long battle over his body between the Indian embassy and Saudi government.

The brick-laying refugee, November 11, 1989

My two Kurdish friends and I worked together, watched each other's back, and lived in the construction zone. We slept

on the roof tops, hiding from local police and Iranian mercenaries. The Kurdish contractor looked after us and took us to
his house for meals and paid us for our work. **The Lord was
still there.**

My Sikh friends and I in UAE, November 11, 1989

I read my Bible and kept up with my growth and witnessed
to my friends, but I did not know about any church in the UAE
to attend.

One day, I was working for an Arab sheik in a small Arab
town, repairing light fixtures. An old friend of mine from 1988
when I worked for the Islamic government as an administrator
in the military hospital project, showed up to my job site. I was
surprised to see him there. I had witnessed to him about Christ
and salvation. I asked him, "How did you find me?" He said, "It
was not too hard; everybody knows you." I asked him, "What
are you doing here?" He said he came to receive what I have. I

asked him again, "What?" He said, "Peace and salvation." So, I led him to Christ, and he went home in peace as a child of God.

He had heard the truth, and the truth brought him out of Iran to a strange country, spending his time and money to receive Christ, the way, the truth, and the life.

Isaiah 55:10–11 NIV says:

> **As the rain and snow come down from heaven, and do not return to it without watering the earth and making it bud and flourish, so that it yields seed for the sower and bread for the eater, so is my word that goes out from my mouth: It will not return to me empty, but will accomplish what I desire and achieve the purpose for which I sent it.**

One day, I was at the construction office collecting my paycheck, and an Egyptian secretary told me about a church nearby. The following Friday, it was Christmas celebration 1990 when I attended church in AL-Ain for the first time.

I was happy to hear the Word of the Lord again and practice my English. It was a church on the side of the mission hospital. The church attendees were of different nationalities, Indians, Arabs, British, Americans, Pakistanis, Sudanese, and Filipinos, and they were friendly toward me.

One of the missionaries in the church took me for dinner and heard my testimony. The following week, one of my church friends from Iran joined me. The missionaries helped us and gave us accommodation and food to eat.

We attended Arabic, English, Filipino, and Pakistani churches. The Arabic church members helped us to find jobs, the English church gave us accommodation for a while until the Filipino church members took us to their home and loved us. It was very comforting to see the church in action and how the Lord takes care of His children.

We read in Isaiah 41:10 NIV, "So, do not fear, for I am with you; do not be dismayed, for I am your God. I will strengthen you and help you; I will uphold you with my righteous right hand."

We painted the exterior and interior building for Arab sheiks and witnessed the wealthy Arab lifestyle and how nomad Arabs of the 1960s now were living in huge palaces with Filipino, Indian, Bengali, Indonesian, Syrian, and Lebanese maids, serving them like slaves. The rate of abuse was astronomical, ranging from physical, sexual, emotional, and psychological. Many of them would commit suicide because of abuse. Some of the maids could speak English and would tell us their dissatisfaction and rage, but they had no choice. Their passports were taken away from them, and their wages were withheld until the end of their contract. They had no access to their family back in their homeland. As I talked to them, they would shed tears.

The Lord put in my heart to do something about it. I went to the Filipino embassy and shared the abuse with the Filipino ambassador, and she said that she could not do anything about it because the maids were brought to the UAE through an agency and of their own free will, and unless there was an official complaint, she could not take any action. I offered my help and the Filipino church support to take the maids to Filipino families so the maids could file a complaint, then the embassy would request the maids' passports and their belongings, plus their salaries and send them home. We saved several Filipino maids' lives from abuse, but there were so many in need of help, especially Indians, Bengalese, and Sri Lankans.

We stayed in the construction zone where we worked. We witnessed the rich Muslim Arab building owners bring their maids into the building under construction and rape them in broad daylight away from their wives. It was disgusting to no end.

The missionary whom I had shared my testimony with had gone back to the USA and shared our story with a Christian organization in the USA, and they prepared a file for us to be presented to the United Nations for refugee status. Another missionary helped us fill the United Nations refugee application, and this time, we managed to present our case to the United Nations.

We entered the UN office and handed our applications to the secretary who was an Egyptian Muslim female. She read through and told me, "How dare you change your religion?" I told her, "Ma'am, with all due respect, that is not your business." She asked me to leave, and I resisted. As we were arguing back and forth, a man came out of his office to see what the commotion was all about, and I told him my story. He rebuked the secretary and asked us to wait. We waited for twenty minutes, and he came out apologizing for the secretary's behavior and told me that he was an Egyptian Muslim but his job was to attend the people who were in need of shelter. He said that we had come at the right time. There were two thousand people ahead of us, and normally, he came three times a year to interview them, but since we were there, he would interview us. We told him our stories, and he promised to give us an answer in a week. After a week, we had our answer and were accepted as refugees.

Psalm 18: 43 NKJV says, "You have delivered me from the strivings of the people; You have made me the head of the nations; A people I have not known shall serve me."

We were told by our friends in the US that once we had our refugee status, we could have our interview with the US immigration office for religious asylum, and they would help us to our new homeland. The nearest US immigration office was in India or Pakistan to which we could not get a visa, and we had no other alternative.

We read through the **B**asic **I**nstructions **B**efore **L**eaving Earth, the **BIBLE,** in **Psalm 27:13-14 NIV, "I remain confident of this: I will see the goodness of the LORD in the land of the living. Wait for the LORD; be strong and take heart and wait for the LORD."**

So, we decided to wait for the Lord.

We kept working and witnessing. I took a computer DOS programming course and witnessed to my Syrian instructor, and he accepted Jesus as his Lord and Savior. In the cool of the night, we used to play volleyball with local Arabs, including one police officer, and I used to witness to them.

I expanded my territory and went to different towns and held Bible study with Indians and Persian Muslims. As I witnessed, I needed Bibles to hand out, but there were not many Bibles to go around. I went to an American pastor who had been in the UAE for a long time and asked for his help, but he said it was against the law to bring Bibles to UAE. So, we prayed for Bibles.

In August 1990, Saddam Hussein attacked Kuwait, and a month later, the American military landed in the UAE, and after defeating Saddam Hussein's army, the US Army chaplain came to our church and gave us 10,000 Gideon Bibles in English, **and all I could say was, "Thank you, Jehovah Jireh."**

I distributed the Bibles in the Catholic church with the priest's blessings to everyone who did not have a Bible, and I witnessed to the priest and asked him many questions to which he did not have answers. I offered to have Bible study, and he challenged me to lead the Bible study.

Not having any experience in Bible teaching, I came to my American pastor in a panic. He calmed me down and gave me Matthew Henry's Commentary and told me how to prepare the lessons. I prepared the lessons, his secretary typed and made multiple copies for me, and by God's grace, I taught the Bible study in the Catholic church with the Catholic priest and thirteen other members of the church.

I needed Arabic Bibles to hand out to Arabic-speaking people, but I had no Arabic Bible. One Friday after church, I noticed an elderly in his mid-seventies standing behind a table with Arabic Bibles to sell. I approached him and asked him about Arabic Bibles and how to get them. He said he would mail them to me from Cyprus, ten Bibles at a time, using the postal service. I told him about the UAE laws, and he said, "The Lord will make it happen," and told me how he smuggled Bibles to Muslim countries for years.

I lived with an Egyptian friend who worked for the mission hospital as a receptionist. We decided to move to the country of Oman, where we had more freedom to share the gospel. In Oman, we managed to receive Bibles using the postal service. One day, the postman knocked on the door and handed me my package, but the package had been opened and he said, "Friend, I opened your package and noticed the Bibles, and I took one. I hope it is ok with you." At first, I thought that we are caught because the postman worked for the government. Then he said, "If it is all right with you, I can take one more for my friend." I gave him another one. From that moment, the post man became my Bible distributor. **The Lord works in mysterious ways.**

Isaiah 55:8-11 NKJV says, "For My thoughts are not your thoughts, nor are your ways My ways, says the Lord. For as the heavens are higher than the earth, so are My ways higher than your ways, and My thoughts than your thoughts."

As our Bible study and discipleship grew, one of our Persian ex-Muslim members was ready to be baptized, and I asked my American pastor to baptize him, but he said it was against the law to baptize an ex-Muslim, but he could come and give his testimony. The new disciple gave his testimony, and I offered to participate in his baptism so I would take the blame for it, and it was agreed.

There was a Somalian worker in the hospital that I was witnessing to, who was a spy for the UAE government. He had taken our pictures and reported us to the UAE police.

The next day, I was called to the police station to give account for my action. The police officer demanded my friend's name and address, but I declined. He threatened to take me to prison, and I offered myself to go to prison, then he threatened to kill me, but I did not budge, and I told him that he could not harm me unless my Father in heaven give him the permission to do so. He asked me, "Who is your father?" and I told him, "God is my father." He asked, "How did God become your father?" And as I was explaining how and when God became my father, he got angry and told me to get out of his office, and I was free.

I came back to my pastor's office; he was surprised that I was not arrested. I told him the story, and he said that I was a troublemaker and needed to leave the country before it got worse.

Chapter Fifteen

Deported Three Times in Two Days

My pastor took my friend and I to immigration court, and we were ordered by the court to leave the country. My friend's visa was still active, and he did not have any trouble leaving the country, but I was told to go, pack my belongings, and check into jail to be processed and deported.

We planned to fly to Yugoslavia and cross the border to West Germany, meet with the US immigration office and from there, we could fly to the USA, our last destination.

The church purchased our air tickets, and on September 25, 1991 at midnight, I arrived at the jail door to be processed. The jail officer opened the jail door, and I went in. From behind the bars, I told my pastor, who had accompanied me, referring to him as my brother, that I would meet him in three hours. The officer turned around and asked me about my conversation with my pastor, and I told him that I would see my brother in three hours. He said, "Is he your brother?" And I said, "Yes." He looked at my pastor, who was green-eyed with white hair, and looked at me who was brown-eyed with black hair, and said, "You don't look alike," and I said, "Correct, we are from the same father but different mother. He came and opened the jail door and pulled me out, saying that he could not keep somebody in jail who had an American brother and apologized, saying, "Please forgive me and go to the airport, and I will bring your passport in three hours so you can leave." **I remembered the verse in Psalm 34:7 NIV, saying, "The angel of the Lord encamps around those who fear him, and he delivers them."**

On Sept. 26, 1991 at 3:00a.m., we left UAE with a stop in Bulgaria, then to Yugoslavia, our destination. All the passengers were allowed into the country except three of us, one Algerian and two Iranians. They told us to turn around and go back to where we came from because there was a civil war going on in Yugoslavia. We were deported to Bulgaria, and Bulgarian authorities tried to send us back to the UAE. We sat down and prayed, and the Lord showed us to go to Turkey.

At the Turkish border in Istanbul, I greeted the immigration officer in the Azeri language (my mother tongue). As he heard me speak in Azeri language, he got up, hugged me, kissed me on both cheeks, and welcomed me as his brother. My friend asked who this guy was, and I told him that the officer was my long-lost cousin, and I did not know it!

We read in Nahum 1:7 NKJV, "The Lord is good, A stronghold in the day of trouble; And He knows those who trust in Him."

In Istanbul, we found the Iranian church and connected with some of the old brothers from Iran. The church was pastored by a retired American missionary to Iran from the 1970s. We participated in worship and building each other's faith.

The American church had supplied our needs by providing us with some financial aid, and we managed to rent a small one-bedroom apartment for four of us, two brothers from Iran and two of us from the UAE. We had a small kitchen and a combination of toilet and shower. The showerhead had an internal heat element that heated the water, and anytime I took a shower, I expected to get electrocuted.

The United Nations office was in Ankara, and by the help of the church in the UAE, we were able to transfer our UN refugee file to Ankara and receive a financial support of one hundred dollars a month. Half of our income was spent on rent, and with the fifty dollars, we survived. We had to exit Turkey every three months to extend our visitor's visa to the neighboring country of Bulgaria and come back.

Bulgaria had just come out of communist control of the Soviet Union after the Soviet Union was dissolved. The country was devastated. We went to the supermarket and found the shelves empty. People were hungry and without jobs. We sat in the hotel lobby and witnessed to Persian refugees. One night, we witnessed an angry mother attacking the hotel attendee, demanding the whereabouts of her daughter. She was a big-sized woman who grabbed the hotel attendee by the neck and said, "I ask you one more time, where is my daughter?" He told her about her daughter in a certain room in the hotel, who was participating in prostitution. The mother went to the room, grabbed her daughter, and while she was beating her, she took her home.

While in Ankara, I helped refugees to put their applications for refugee status together in English and witnessed to the refugees. Iranian refugees in Ankara were in dire need, spiritually and physically. These were the members of the different political groups who helped Khomeini's regime to achieve victory over Shah and take over the country but were then rejected by the Islamic regime. Some of them were the people loyal to the Shah regime. They were hungry, wounded, broken, and in need of a Savior. We witnessed to them and took some of them to the doctor, cleaned them up, and found jobs so they could feed themselves.

We found a skinny young man, bent over with infected kidneys; a son of a military general, who was killed by the Islamic regime, took him to the doctor and fed him. We prepared his application to the UN, and he received his refugee status. After his recovery, he gave his life to Christ and worked in the church until the UN found a country to accept him.

My friend got a job in the UN as a translator, and we separated our ways. I joined with another brother in the church and started a ministry to feed the refugee families. We would buy sacks of food and deliver them to the front door of the refugee families, and few of them came to church and surrendered their lives to Jesus.

We did not have much money to buy quality food with enough nourishment and as a result, my friend's wife had a miscarriage. Sometimes we would find cheap fish by the black seashore, but mostly we ate canned food.

My US missionary friend had found a sponsor for me so I could come to the US as a permanent resident. In March 16, 1992, I was called by the US embassy to go to the hospital for a physical examination, and I passed the test. A Christian organization had purchased my air tickets as a loan so I could pay them back later, and on June 8, 1992, I left Turkey for my final destination, **the United States of America.**

Chapter Sixteen

A Sojourner in a Strange Country

⸻ ⋅◦⟡◦⋅ ⸻

On June 10, 1992, at 12 p.m., I arrived in Tulsa Oklahoma Airport. I was sitting around the carousel and waiting for my luggage to arrive. I had a strange feeling, and I asked the Lord, "What am I doing here, Lord? Why did you bring me to this God-forsaken country? What is my purpose here?" And I kept quiet. Then I heard a voice, saying, "**I will send you house to house.**" I asked, "What am I supposed to do?" And the voice said, "**Keep talking.**"

I did not understand. How was I supposed to go house to house, and what was I supposed to say?

As a militant Muslim, I had studied the American Constitution, American politics, CIA activities around the world and in Iran, the Vietnam War, and so on because I believed that in a battle, I needed to know my enemy better than my friend, and **I had considered Imperialist America as an enemy.** Everybody in the world considers America, the promised land; that is why they flock into this country for freedom and opportunities to prosper, but for me, it was different. I felt like Jonah, saying, "Lord, don't you know what have they done to my country, Iran? They destroyed it. My people are scattered all over the world. Their policies have turned my country to a heap of ruin. And now, You want me to do what? Go into their houses and say what?"

The soft and small voice of the Lord whispered into my ear, **"Love your enemy; you are here to glorify My name."**

Culture Shock

My sponsor came and took me to his house, and the next day, he gave me a job in his business as a carpet shampooing man and allowed me to stay in his apartment until I had enough money to rent on my own. **I had only three dollars to my name.** I went to Safeway next door to buy a loaf of bread. I had not seen a Safeway that big. There were aisles after aisles six feet high, and I felt that I was looking for a needle in a haystack.

As I was looking for bread, I found myself in an aisle of packaged food with animal pictures on them, and I asked the attendant the reason for the animal pictures, and she said, "That is animal food." I asked her, "You mean that you process food for animals and package it too?" She said, "What is wrong with that?" And I said, "There is a lot wrong with that. My people in Iran, cannot find food for themselves, let alone for their animals." And to make matters worse, she showed me the animal hospital across the street. I had only one thing to say to her, "Ma'am, you have a lot to be grateful for. I suggest that you get on your knees and praise the One who gave you so much." And she smiled and showed me the aisle for real bread. **That was my first culture shock.**

I worked for my sponsor for four months at $4.25 per hour, washing carpets and working in his antique shop. My first check was $600.00, and I thought that was a lot of money. I took it to the bank to open an account, and the bank refused to open an account for me because I had no credit. I asked them, "What is credit?" They told me that I needed to buy all I needed on credit and pay later, so I could build credit. I told the bank teller that was a debt, not credit, and she said, "You got that one right; **America is a debt-based society.** And I asked my sponsor to help me to open an account with the bank, and **that was my second culture shock.**

I attended his small church until I found a better-paying job, and I moved on. I had many skills, but none of them was US-certified. With the help of church members, I signed up for heating and air conditioning night school in November 1992 and finished school by September 1993 as a heating and air conditioning technician.

I did not speak fluent English and took two dictionaries along with my school book to school. My instructor told me that I would not make it through the school and would fail because it was a compressed study of three years of school offered in eleven months, and I told him, "Sir, you teach, and I learn. If I fail, that will be my problem," but I did not know the reason for his comment until the end of school that he did not like me because I was from Iran, and he told me that he hated my guts.

I finished school as an honor graduate, and instructors and American students walked away at the graduation party because a foreigner (non-Oklahoman) had reached the top, and they left all the pizzas and drinks behind. The school principal apologized as he handed me my certificates, and I took all the pizzas and drinks home and distributed them among

133

my neighbors. **This was my first experience of American discrimination.**

I asked the school principal for my instructors' home address, and he declined for fear of retaliation by me. I assured him that I wanted to take a gift to him and thank him for his great teaching skills. He gave me the address hesitantly.

I went to my instructor's house and knocked on the door. He opened the door, and seeing me, he was taken back, and with an angry voice, said, "What are you doing here?" I said, "Sir, I bear a gift, and it is to appreciate you for being a great instructor." He said, "I don't want your gift." I said, "May I come in?" He said, "No." At this time, his wife came to the door trying to find out what the noise was all about. When I saw her, I told her my reason for being there. She invited me in, and her husband said, "He has ten minutes." She said, "Why?" And he said, "I hate his guts; his people took our people hostage," referring to Iranian students taking American embassy people hostage.

She showed me a seat, and I sat down. My instructor was a Navy veteran. I said, "Permission to speak, sir?" He said, "Go for it." I said, "Sir, if have wronged you, I ask for your forgiveness, but I think I am not the problem; rather, you are. May I ask what is it that bothers you? As far as I know, I always respected you." He said, "None of your business. Are you a doctor?" I said, "No, but I am child of God; I can pray for you." He said, "Are you a Jehovah Witness or Latter-Day Saints?" I said, "No, let me tell you who I am."

I said, "There was a mighty lion in the jungle, and every animal respected him. One day, Mr. Lion stepped on a thorn bush, and a piece of thorn got lodged into his paw. He was on the ground and roaring in pain, and nobody could approach him, and everybody was scared of him. There came a little mouse and saw the crowd gathered around the lion in the middle. He carefully approached and looked at the lion and said: 'Mr. Lion, may I see your paw,' and the lion roared and tried to catch the mouse, but the mouse was too little and fast. The little mouse said again, 'Mr. Lion, if you show me your paw, I will take care of your pain.' The lion agreed, and using his tiny teeth, the little mouse removed the thorn from his paw; the pain was gone, and everybody, including the lion, were relieved."

I told my instructor, "I am that little mouse, and you are the lion." He kept silent, and his wife continued and said, "We have a son who is paralyzed, and there is no help for him, and that bothers my husband and makes him angry."

I asked my instructor if I can hold his hand, and he allowed me to hold his hand, and I prayed for him. He started sobbing and told me he had not met anyone like me. **And there I was, going house to house and talking as the Lord told me at the airport on June 10, 1992 at 12 p.m.. And I found my purpose in America sharing the Lord's love and compassion with His lost sheep.**

I finished my apprenticeship program with a small company in Oklahoma and moved to Oregon for better job opportunities on July 4, 1996. I worked for another small company until I learned local codes, and in April 1999, I started my own heating and air conditioning company called Faith HVAC, Inc. I purchased a truck and my tools with a loan from the bank, and got a printer and printed 15,000 flyers, and distributed them door to door on foot to create a customer base.

Two weeks into my newly established business, I took on my church school gymnasium heating and air conditioning project and made enough money to pay off all my debts.

I started going house to house as a heating and air conditioning service man. And every house I entered, my customer would ask me the question, "Who are you? Where are you from, and what is your story?" And there I went again, **going house to house and talking,** and I have been sharing my testimony and how the Lord has brought me out of the darkness of Islam into His magnificent light.

There is a hefty price to pay when someone leaves Satan's dominion and joins God's kingdom. I and several others became Satan's target. Our lives, properties, and health were affected.

On January 19, 1994, our church leader who defended our right to worship the Lord in Iran was kidnapped, stabbed many times, and killed by the Islamic government to silence the voice of Christ in Iran. They had buried him in an unknown grave. After a month searching for him, his son managed to identify him and recovered his body. But despite government effort to suffocate the church, the number of new believers from Muslim background had increased from a few hundred in the 1970s to millions today.

Christ said in Matthew 10:38, "And whoever does not take his cross and follow me is not worthy of me. Whoever finds his life will lose it, and whoever loses his life for my sake will find it."

I lived a semi-normal life until 1999 when I developed severe internal bleeding from my stomach down to my colon after I took my first flu shot.

I had bloody diarrhea, stomach pain, a bleeding ulcer, and colitis on top of a fever and chills. Doctors performed an endoscopy, colonoscopy, chest and brain scan, blood tests, and did all they could and diagnosed me with ulcerative colitis and put me on heavy steroids to stop the bleeding and inflammation, and a handful of drugs.

Today, by the grace of God, I am healed from most of the internal diseases I had, but I still have fever, chills, and heavy sweats, so I drink a lot of water to keep hydrated and shave my head to keep cool. At night, I get fever and chills every two hours, and I get up, cool my head down, walk around for few minutes, and go back to sleep. When I talk, my mouth dries up, and I need to drink water at all times. **In all these, I give thanks to the Lord who gave me life, sustained me throughout these years, and made me His ambassador to the nations.**

I preach the good news of Christ to Americans because it is the power of God to salvation for everyone who believes. I have no intention to convert anyone nor any power to do so but to introduce them to the truth Himself, Jesus Christ, who offers them freedom from their sins and living water for life to drink.

I share the gospel with Muslims using their religious book to start the conversation so they will know that I don't mean to introduce them to another religion but to the way, the truth, and the life that they have been praying for. They have been praying to be led to the straight path, not knowing that the straight path is not some road to travel on, but the straight path is someone who they need to walk with whose name is Jesus.

I want the Muslims to know that Jesus died for them too, not because He was one of three Gods of Christianity, but He was God in the flesh who came and died for their sins too, so the Muslims do not have to die to reach God, but God died for them to reconcile them with Himself.

A Witness to the Nation

As I went along doing business and witnessing, I realized that the Lord had brought me to the US for a purpose of evangelizing Americans. After I told my story to my customers, I was invited to their church to share my testimony with their congregation, and I started to teach the church how to share the gospel with the Muslim neighbors.

For me, Americans were already Christians, and they did not need me telling them about Christ, but the Lord showed me that they are the same people in darkness as Muslims, regardless of ethnicity.

But wait, how about all those massive churches decorated inside and outside with pastors and bishops of so many degrees around this country? I went and listened to the PHD (Post Hole Digger)-holding pastor's sermon; with all due respect to PHD, I found them divided, and everybody beats different drum. They are pompous, arrogant, and proud. They show up in their holy garments, with shiny big rings on their fingers, high and lifted up, and claiming that they worked so hard preparing the message. When they speak, they brag about their Greek and Hebrew language degree, and their names contain so many prefixes. **They have compromised and watered down the truth. They do not condemn nor confront sin.**

They go along to get along with the world. Many churches do not even have an altar call to invite sinners to repent and accept the gift of salvation through Christ Jesus, and if there is an altar call, they say, "Please come forward so we can pray for you." Their message does not convict the sinner to come forward for repentance; rather, it is lukewarm and pleasing to the ears of the sinner. To capture their audience, they philosophize the gospel and make it hard to understand, and to understand their sermon, you need to have dictionaries to get the gist of their sermon. **Humility is a rare commodity and sometimes nonexistent.**

The church has to wake up and make the choice to serve and follow the Lord or worship at the feet of Baal.

The church in the West is well-structured. Pastors are well-trained and well-groomed, the pews are nice and clean, the buildings are air-conditioned, the choir is well-rehearsed, and the hymnals are set, but overall, most of the churches are like a sounding brass or clanging cymbal.

To me, the church in the West is like a well-trained army, arrayed in battle, equipped with all the necessary guns and ammunitions, but comes short of pulling the trigger to destroy the enemy and, instead, the enemy carries out the attack and destroys them, and then the church turns around and blames the government for their shortcomings.

My grandfather was an illiterate farmer but very wise. He told me as the fruit tree bears more fruits, its branches lower their head down because of the weight of fruits, and the farmer can access the fruits, but the non-fruit-bearing tree has its head in the air flying high. This was his way of telling me that as I gain knowledge, expertise, and wealth, I should be humble and down to earth so people can benefit from me, and he added, the taller the tree, the harder the fall and greater the damage.

Jesus said in Matthew 23:12, "Whoever exalts himself will be humbled, and whoever humbles himself will be exalted."

After the church service, they may extend their hands without even acknowledging the person. They forgot that they are supposed to be a shepherd, yet they do not know how to shepherd two sheep. Shepherding is not an easy job. It requires hard work and sleepless nights. It is dirty and stressful.

When a sheep is left behind with a broken leg, the shepherd has to put the sheep on his shoulder, carrying the weight of the sheep, plus putting up with the smelly underbelly of the sheep, then he has to care for the sheep until the sheep recovers. They admire the Good Shepherd Jesus and prepare great sermons about Him, but they don't lift a finger to be a good shepherd. When a member of the church calls for help, unless the member has a prefix to his or her name, that member will be ignored, or they will get to that member sometime later.

The church in the West is playing religion, and that is the main reason the church is dying and church buildings are sold to be a Mosque or dance room in the neighborhood. It is not the fault of the world for being dark; rather, it is the light of the church that is getting dimmer and dimmer.

Jesus, in John 10:11–14, says:

> **I am the good shepherd. The good shepherd lays down his life for the sheep. He who is a hired hand and not a shepherd, who does not own the sheep, sees the wolf coming and leaves the sheep and flees, and the wolf snatches them and scatters them. He flees because he is a hired hand and cares nothing for the sheep. I am the good shepherd. I know my own and my own know me.**

Unity is scarce in the Christian communities. The churches are full of well-dressed Sunday Christians but come Monday, nobody knows who they are because they all are blended in with the people of darkness. ***Camouflage is no longer a military term but Christian.*** I looked for light; there was none. I searched for salt; it was hardly there. Many of the pastors preach what the Bible calls itching of ears. **Politically correct sermons have run amuck in American churches. The good is called evil, and evil is called good.**

We read in 2 Timothy 4:2–4:

> **Preach the word; be ready in season and out of season; reprove, rebuke, and exhort, with complete patience and teaching. For the time is coming when people will not endure sound teaching, but having itching ears they will accumulate for themselves teachers to suit their own passions, and will turn away from listening to the truth and wander off into myths.**

When I arrived in this country, I expected to see the light and the salt, but instead, I saw mere humans whose hearts have gone after different gods. Paganism is rampant more than ever. **Greed, pride and selfishness, immorality, and even ungodliness has taken over the church.** Neighbor does not know his neighbor, let alone try to love him. Even in many churches, the person who sits next to you does not bother to get to know you because of your different skin color or ethnicity.

Jesus said in Mark 3:25, "And if a house is divided against itself, that house will not be able to stand."

The church has lost its compass and bearing and spinning without control. It has crossed into the land of apostasy, and some are gone too far off that they passed the point of no return.

We read in 1 Peter 4:17-18 NIV, "For it is time for judgment to begin with God's household; and if it begins with us, what will the outcome be for those who do not obey the Gospel of God? And, if it is hard for the righteous to be saved, what will become of the ungodly and the sinner?"

American churches are becoming more secular and accommodating sin, which is contrary to the gospel of truth. It is time that the church follows the correction given by the Lord in 2 Chronicles 7:14, **"If my people who are called by my name humble themselves, and pray and seek my face and turn from their wicked ways, then I will hear from heaven and will forgive their sin and heal their land."**

And after doing that, it takes each truly born-again believer in Christ to disciple one person a year to turn this magnificent country to the Lord. Sharing testimonies and praises in the big churches are no longer popular because the Dr. Pastor has to present his jargon-full sermon. I have tried to share my testimony in big churches and, for the most part, I faced resistance from the Dr. Pastor. I have been called a Christian fanatic or am too bold.

One Saturday, I was called to repair an air conditioner belonging to an old customer of mine who was a judge. On a regular maintenance procedure, I would only see his wife, but this time on Saturday, she was out shopping, and his honor was home. My company was called Faith HVAC, Inc., and I had a big fish symbol on the side of my truck.

As usual, I greeted my customer and went along with the repair. It was a simple repair, and I finished it before his honor managed to come and supervise me. I wrote the invoice, and he wrote me a check, and as he was handing me the check, he pointed to the fish sign on my service truck and asked, "What does that fish mean?" He was a judge, and I expected him to know the meaning of the fish for being an early second and third-century Christian symbol to recognize each other because of persecution, but nevertheless, he squeezed me. I replied that it was my Christian belief symbol. He said, "So, you believe that there is a God who created you?" I said, "Your Honor, I don't just believe, I know because He is my Father." He said, "Young man, that is the figment of your imagination; there is no God."

I continued, "Your Honor, you are a judge." He said, "Tell me something I don't know." I said, "Please bear with me. There is a law that is understood among Muslims that if their children behave in an unworthy manner toward God and commit the unforgivable sin of adultery between brother and sister, the father has the right to kill them both, and it is **called honor killing**. Let's say that man is been brought to your court. How would you judge him?" He said, "Guilty." I said, "Not so fast. He has done right by his religion; you don't have the right to condemn him." He said, "What he has done is wrong." I said, "What defines wrong?" He said, "We have right and wrong; is that hard to understand?" I said, "No, Your Honor, I totally understand, but what defines right?" He said, "Son, that is an acceptable truth." I said, "What defines truth?" He said, "I don't know." I went on and said, "Your Honor, this is what I know: the truth, and right and wrong are defined by **the moral**

law, and **the moral law** has a **moral law giver,** whose name is **God,** who is my Father."

He looked at me and said, "Young man, I asked you to come and repair my air conditioner, not to stump me." I said, "Your Honor, I meant no disrespect to you, but I only answered your question. Have a blessed day."

Chapter Seventeen

The Cost of Accepting Christ

T here is a difference between knowing about Christ and knowing Him personally, and at times, I found that it is easy to witness to a Muslim or pagan than to an American who is a so-called Christian.

Most Muslims are seekers after God, but they are looking for Him in the wrong places and wrong identity, and all they need is to be directed to the right path who is Jesus, the way, the truth, and the life. Muslims identify God as **Allah, who is a pre-Islamic Nabataeans pagan moon god and has its roots in Babylon during King Nabonidus (556–536 BC). They called this moon god, Nannar.**

The western church has identity crises. They forgot that they are supposed to be workers in the field to bring the harvest home; instead, they are in a magnificent building preaching feel-good sermons.

In 1995, I received a call from an old friend I had met in Turkey whose family's lives were in danger. They had left Turkey and had gone back to Iran, but the Iranian government had been monitoring their activities among Muslims. I made contact with our friends in the US and sponsored them as refugees, so they could come to US. They came to the US, started a ministry, and invited me to share my testimony on live TV broadcasting to Iran in the Farsi language. Before I had my interview with my friend to tell my story, the program director asked me to choose a name. I told him, "I have a name, the same name my father gave me before he died." He said, "Not that one; we need to give you a different name to disguise you for your protection, and I said, "The **Bible says in Psalm 119:114 NIV, "You are my refuge and my shield; I have put my hope in your word**," and I told him, "When I gave my life to Jesus, He promised to protect me from the enemy Satan, and no one can snatch me from Jesus's hand." My story went for one hour and was broadcasted to Iran, and my nieces and nephew had watched it.

When I accepted Christ Jesus as my Lord and Savior, I totally understood Christ's Lordship over me, meaning He, Jesus, King of kings and Lord of lords, has become my Lord and King, and no one on earth, under earth, above earth, or anywhere else has power over Him. Jesus conquered fear and death for me by dying on the cross and rising from the dead, and **He told me over and over: "Do not fear, for I am with you. I will uphold you with My right hand. I am your shield. I am your shepherd**."

My pastor in Iran told me about the consequence of my new life in Christ that I may be disowned by my family, and I told him, "It has already happened." He told me my family would abandon me, and I told him, "That has happened already too." I was not dependent on anything of this world. They could not threaten me with my inheritance; it was already taken from me. They could not threaten me with my life because I had almost been dead. They could not scare me by taking away my job because I had none. And when I look back, I understand that the Lord had been preparing me for this before I was born.

Apostle John in 1 John 2:15–17, says:

Do not love the world or the things in the world. If anyone loves the world, the love of the Father is not in him. For all that is in the world—the desires of the flesh and the desires of the eyes and pride of life—is not from the Father but is from the world. And the world is passing away along with its desires, but whoever does the will of God abides forever.

So, I was free to join the family of God.

Jesus said in Luke 14:26–27, "If anyone comes to me and does not hate his own father and mother and wife and children and brothers and sisters, yes, and even his own life, he cannot be my disciple. Whoever does not bear his own cross and come after me cannot be my disciple."

I am not saying fear does not exist, but we can overcome fear by faith in Jesus. When I joined the military, we were told that fear is the catalyst for preparedness and in order to defeat the enemy, we needed to learn the enemies' tactics and schemes so we could defend ourselves against them and attack the enemy in an efficient manner. As a soldier, you can have the most sophisticated weapons of war, but unless you are trained on how to put them to use, they will be useless, and you will suffer defeat.

Faith overcomes fear, but where do we get faith? The Bible says in Romans 10:17, **"So faith comes from hearing, and hearing through the word of Christ."** So, we are back to reading the **BIBLE: B**asic **I**nstructions **B**efore **L**eaving **E**arth.

This Is War, Whether We Like It or Not.

As a child of God, we know for sure that we are at war against the archenemy Satan, and we need to know how to put the tools of the spiritual battle to work.

Apostle Paul inspired, by the Holy Spirit, has given us details of the battle in Ephesians 6:10–18:

> Finally, be strong in the Lord and in the strength of his might. Put on the whole armor of God, that you may be able to stand against the schemes of the devil. For we do not wrestle against flesh and blood, but against the rulers, against the authorities, against the cosmic powers over this present darkness, against the spiritual forces of evil in the heavenly places. Therefore, take up the whole armor of God, that you may be able to withstand in the evil day, and having done all, to stand firm. Stand therefore, having fastened on the belt of truth, and having put on the breastplate of righteousness, and, as shoes for your feet, having put on the readiness given by the gospel of peace. In all circumstances take up the shield of faith, with which you can extinguish all the flaming darts of the evil one; and take the helmet of salvation, and the sword of the Spirit, which is the word of God, praying at all times in the Spirit, with all prayer and supplication. To that end, keep alert with

**all perseverance, making supplication for all
the saints.**

I am a foot-soldier of Christ, and Christ is the commander
in chief. He has given me armors of defense to use in the battle
that I am involved in. So, I should fasten the **belt of truth** to
fight Satan's lies, which he dresses up as truths. I should put
on **the breastplate of righteousness of Christ** to protect my
heart, faith, and emotions from the enemy, then I should put
on the **shoes of the gospel of peace,** so I can spread the good
news of the Messiah and His salvation to the people in this
dark world. The next armor is the **shield of faith** that comes
as a gift from Jesus, so I can use to deflect the fiery darts of
Satan, which comes as temptations, accusations, and lies. A
soldier needs a helmet, which is the **helmet of salvation,** to
protect my thoughts against doubts about my salvation in
Christ Jesus. And a soldier needs an offensive tool to attack,
which is **the Word of God** and Word of Truth to use against
Satan as Jesus Himself used and said: "**It is written,**" but to
know what is written, we, as God's foot-soldiers, need to read
His book as our daily bread and store it in our minds to have
it ready when needed.

The Cost of Compromising the Truth

I was getting measurements to design A/C systems for a
church. Hearing a different accent and seeing a different skin
color, the pastor of the church asked me a question about
this country. **I pointed at the abortion law, Roe versus Wade
of January 1973, by which millions of children have been
cut into pieces.** He said, "The Supreme Court did it, and I

responded, "No, the church kept quiet and did not inform the people to object to the ungodly law, so the church is responsible." The pastor was not happy with me, and I did not get the job; instead, they took my idea and gave the job to someone else. Yes, **telling the truth comes with a cost, but are we willing to pay the cost?**

As an immigrant, I look at this country, and it is a magnificent and prosperous country. I cherish the freedom in this country, and the Lord is using this country in many ways to reach out to His lost sheep all over the world, but at the same time, this country has to give an account for its actions toward innocent children. Everybody talks about the **mother's right** or **"my body, my choice"** to abort (destroy) her baby in her womb, but nobody talks about the baby's right to live. Oh, yeah, they call it tissue without life, but wait a minute, if a drunk driver knocks a pregnant mother down with his car, and the mother and baby (tissue) die, it would be considered a double homicide. How in the world did the tissue suddenly come to be a living organ? Who are we kidding? This country will have to answer to God, and the judgment will begin with the house of the Lord.

The Bible is very clear in 1 Corinthians 3:11–15:

> **For no one can lay a foundation other than that which is laid, which is Jesus Christ. Now if anyone builds on the foundation with gold, silver, precious stones, wood, hay, straw— each one's work will become manifest, for the Day will disclose it, because it will be revealed by fire, and the fire will test what sort of work each one has done. If the work that anyone**

has built on the foundation survives, he will
receive a reward. If anyone's work is burned
up, he will suffer loss, though he himself will
be saved, but only as through fire.

In 2 Kings 18, we see that King Hezekiah did everything right
in the eyes of the Lord and removed all the high places and
broke into pieces the bronze snake called **Nehushtan,** which
Moses had made and brought sanity to Judah; then Manasseh,
his son, turned everything upside down and did evil in the eyes
of the Lord like most of the kings of Judah, but he made the
matter worse by **passing his own son through the fire.**

After Manasseh and his son Amon, who did the same as
his father, Josiah became king of Judah, renewed the covenant
with the Lord, and cleaned up the mess that his father and
grandfather committed. And he did everything right according
to the laws of Moses, and **the Bible in 2 Kings 23:26-27, says:**

Still the Lord did not turn from the burning of
his great wrath, by which his anger was kin-
dled against Judah, because of all the provo-
cations with which Manasseh had provoked
him. And the Lord said, "I will remove Judah
also out of my sight, as I have removed Israel,
and I will cast off this city that I have chosen,
Jerusalem, and the house of which I said, My
name shall be there."

So as a foot soldier of the Lord Most High, I beg the church
to come back to the Lord and repent and pray that the Lord
may relent from His fury, restore His house, and heal the

wounds of His people in this country. We read in 2 Chronicles 7:14, **"If my people who are called by my name humble themselves, and pray and seek my face and turn from their wicked ways, then I will hear from heaven and will forgive their sin and heal their land."**

He Is the Potter, We Are the Clay

I always ask this question of the Lord, "Lord, why me? I am just an orphan and inadequate shepherd boy. I don't have any skills nor high education to be used in Your kingdom." The Lord is very gracious in His answer, saying, **"It is not what you are or what you know; rather, it is who you are in Me. I have saved you, and you are My co-worker and My hands and feet to do My work among My lost sheep. You are My ambassador to represent Me as salt and light on earth until I bring you home. I picked you up from miry dirt, cleansed you, and called you My son. I have paid a high price for you, the blood of My only Son. You are Mine, and nobody can snatch you from My hand.**

One cold Friday evening, after my daily routine past five o' clock, as I was driving home, my business phone rang. I did not usually answer the call after five, but this time, I did. The person on the other side said, "Help," and I said, "How may I help you?" Still, the voice said, "Help." It was very strange, so I asked him for his address, and I kept him on the phone so I could get more detailed information about his furnace. By the time I got to his house, I had figured out what the problem was with his furnace, but I still could not figure out the tone of his voice except it was alarming. I asked him to go to the thermostat in the house and turn the furnace on. By the time he came back, I had replaced the part and was on my way to write the invoice. He asked what was wrong, and I showed him the defective part and told him how I fixed it, then he asked me, "Who are you?" **I shared my testimony with him,** and his family was happy that they had heat for the night.

He followed me to my truck and handed me the check. He looked at me with tears in his eyes and said, "Do you know that you were sent by God?" I replied, "Yes sir, I know that." He told me that he was going to commit suicide that night after everybody had gone to bed because he was at the end of his rope, and there was no hope for him. He had called me to repair the furnace so his family could have heat before he could end his life, but hearing my story gave him hope, and he was going to church on Sunday. He said that up until that moment, he thought there was no God, but now he knows there is a loving God who cares for him.

The Lord told me that I am chosen for a purpose. We read in 1 Peter 2:9-10, **"But you are a chosen race, a royal priesthood, a holy nation, a people for his own possession, that you may proclaim the excellencies of him who called you out of darkness into his marvelous light. Once you were not a people, but now you are God's people; once you had not received mercy, but now you have received mercy."**

I had an elderly German, born-again Christian customer whom I served on a regular basis. I was her Yellow Pages. She would call me, even when she needed a painter or handyman. One hot summer evening, she called and asked me to install an air conditioner for her best friend from her high school days. We were booked for the next few weeks, and I said it would be at least two weeks before I could get to him, but she insisted that he was an old man and would die of heat stroke. I managed to rearrange my commercial non-emergency customer and gave him the proposal. He signed the contract, and we ordered the A/C unit.

It was a hot summer afternoon. I assigned part of the work to my employee, and I was running back and forth, and this eighty-year-old man kept following me. I asked him to sit on a chair and watch, but please stay out of my way so we may not collide into each other, and he did. As I was working, I had a hymn on my lips, singing, "**Praise be the Lord, His mercy endures forever and ever.**"

He asked me, "Hey, what are you murmuring about?" I said, "Sir, I am singing," and he asked, "What are you singing about?" I said, "I am singing: Praise be the Lord, His mercy endures forever and ever." He asked, "Who is *Lord*?" I said, "He is my Dad," and I explained how the Lord had become my Dad. And he said, "Whatever," and went inside because it was too hot.

We finished the work, cleaned up, and I gave him the invoice, and he paid me. I said, "Have a nice evening and may the Lord bless you." He was very happy and appreciative, and I left.

A month later, one early Saturday morning, my phone rang, and I picked it up. It was my elderly German lady customer. She said, "Guess what happened?" I said, "What?" She continued, "Remember my old friend you installed the A/C for?" I said, "Yes." She said that her friend was a high school friend, and she had been witnessing to him for a long time, and he always shut her down because he was an atheist, but after I installed his A/C, something happened.

She said he came to help her in the garden, and before he did anything, he opened up his arms in the form of a cross and said to her that he surrendered his life to the one that A/C man believes. She asked him, "Who?" He said, "The A/C man," and she said, "You mean, James," and he said, "Yes. He was happy, singing, trustworthy, clean, and he did not charge me extra because of the hot summer season." Then my customer had led him to Christ.

The old man went home, and a week later, he was gardening in his backyard, had a heart attack, and died. His wife called my old German customer and reported that her husband died. My customer told her that her husband was not dead but with Jesus because she had led him to Christ a week ago. Then my German lady customer went to her house and led her to Christ.

After telling the whole story, my old German lady customer asked me what was my secret that was so effective? I told her **my secret is that I am always ready to give an answer to everyone who asks me the reason for the hope I have in Christ.**

We read in 2 Timothy 1:8-9, "**Therefore do not be ashamed of the testimony about our Lord, nor of me his prisoner, but share in suffering for the gospel by the power of God, who saved us and called us to a holy calling, not because of our works but because of his own purpose and grace, which he gave us in Christ Jesus before the ages began.**"

Apostle Paul is advising young Timothy of his holy calling. How can a believer stay holy in an unholy world to carry out a mission that the Lord has in mind for the believer? The Bible has an answer for it.

We read in Leviticus 20:7–8, "**Consecrate yourselves, therefore, and be holy, for I am the Lord your God. Keep my statutes and do them; I am the Lord who sanctifies you.**"

My grandmother had a polished steel mirror, and after a while, we no longer could see our faces in it. Then we would hear the polishing man yelling on the street, and Grandfather would pay him to polish it again so we could see our faces again.

The polisher would use certain chemicals, fine sand, and scrub it for a while, then mirror would be a mirror again.

We as believers get rusty and dirty by the affairs of this world as we go through it, and we need to go to the Lord on a daily basis in prayer to be cleaned and sanctified by Him and get ready for the next day's holy calling, so He can be glorified through us. To be cleansed by the Lord, we need to humble ourselves before Him, lay down our pride, and surrender to Him completely, so He can scrub our filth, guilt and make us new again.

We read in James 4:10, **"Humble yourselves before the Lord, and he will exalt you."**

The Bible is not a chronicle nor a biography, but it is an unfolding of God's plan of redemption, how we are to be saved.

When I came to God through the redemptive blood of Jesus Christ, which was paid as a ransom for my sins, I became an asset in the hand of Almighty God. I am no longer just a person who lives on this earth for my pleasure but for God's pleasure. Therefore, what I do, say, and how I live my life has to please Him.

Hebrews 11:6 NIV says, "And without faith it is impossible to please God, because anyone who comes to him must believe that he exists and that he rewards those who earnestly seek him."

Muslims are the same people who are created in God's image, but because of their upbringing in Islam, they live in darkness under the control of the prince of darkness, Satan. How can we help the Muslims out of the darkness? It is by being a light to them, so they can follow the light in us out of their dark lives. You see, we cannot blame the Muslims for being in the dark; rather, we need to look inside of us to find out if our light is on or not. What makes it possible for a person to come out of the darkness, is for the light to shine in the distance, so the person in the dark can follow the light out of darkness.

In September 2009, I joined rank with a ministry that ministers to Muslims on Satellite TV. I built a metallic structure to mount cameras and lights for TV production. We produced many programs as a dialogue between a Muslim and Christian pastor who has the knowledge of Quran and broadcasted through satellite TV. Many Muslims have surrendered their lives to Jesus through that ministry.

Evangelism to Muslims Is an Individual Ministry.

Even though the message of salvation in Christ Jesus, His death, and resurrection are the same, the approach is different. There are cultural, ideological, linguistic, and sociological barriers between Christians and Muslims. A servanthood attitude is usually a good start to develop friendship to gain their trust and show Christlike love and care that they are important in the eyes of God who gave His Son to die for the redemption of their sins. We, as children of God, are set apart to be a witness to the people around us.

We read in Jeremiah 1:5 NKJV, "Before I formed you in the womb I knew you; Before you were born I sanctified you; I ordained you a prophet to the nations."

Chapter Eighteen

New Mission Field

For a long time, good-hearted American missionaries with a holy calling learned many foreign languages, cultures, acquired many skills, raised finances, and took their families along to a strange and hostile country to be witnesses to a Muslim family next door in order to win them to Christ, and in the process, many lost their lives. Satan wants to keep Muslims under his demonic power, and in the late 1970s, missionaries were pushed out of many Muslim countries due to the Islamic revolution and political unrests. But God loves Muslims the same way He loves the rest of the world.

Many Muslims migrated to the West in what we call the **Muslim diaspora** and became our neighbors. Now for the Muslims, the new country is a strange and hostile country. They came to find freedom, but they have a bad taste toward the Christian family next door from their past upbringing in Islam; plus, what they see in the neighborhood is not something to brag about. Christians in the West are not a good witness to the new Muslim neighbor.

They see unbridled licentiousness and immorality, dishonesty and injustice, drug infestation, Hollywood movies, alcohol in grocery stores, pornography, gender confusion, and gang activities. Muslims look at their neighbor, trying to find what they have been missing. The burden is on the Christian neighbor to show why Christ is the "all righteous one" and what His life and sacrificial death accomplished by paying the penalty of sin forever, and whosoever believes in Him will have eternal life.

We read in Ezekiel 36:23, "**And I will vindicate the holiness of my great name, which has been profaned among the nations, and which you have profaned among them. And the nations will know that I am the Lord, declares the Lord God, when through you I vindicate my holiness before their eyes.**"

Muslims believe in eternal punishment. Quran 16:61 says: "If Allah were to punish men for their wrong doing, He would not leave (On the earth) a single living creature." And we read in the Romans 3:23, "For all have sinned and fall short of the glory of God.

And also, in Romans 6:23, "For the wages of sin is death, *but* **the free gift of God is eternal life in Christ Jesus our Lord."**

The mission field has been relocated from foreign country to next door. It is no longer necessary to learn a strange language nor culture. Muslims are here and learning our language and customs. **It is time for us as God's chosen people to be a light and salt to the Muslim next door.** We are that instrument, which God has chosen to illuminate the mind of man. As the sun comes out in the morning and the darkness of the night escapes, so are we to enter this dark world and illuminate it with the word of our testimonies. Our fuel to burn our light is the Word of Truth that flows through us by the power of the Holy Spirit.

As strangers, Muslims are looking for a friend they can trust. They have no peace and have a hard time smiling. Their home country is in disarray, and now they have to learn a new language and culture to survive. God has a purpose for them too, and **our job is to be a Christ to them.** In a way, we are salesmen for Christ. We have access to the precious commodity of salvation, peace, joy, healing, and eternal life through Christ Jesus that we need to advertise through our lives and testimony as a witness to the people around us, especially to Muslims next door.

I traveled to Kauai for vacation, a small island in the Pacific Ocean. I went all over the island, especially to the highlands, and noticed roosters and hens all over the island. I asked locals about it, and they told me that there was a tornado in the island that passed through the chicken farm and picked the chickens and roosters up and spread them all over the island, and it was not possible to gather them back to the farm, **so Kauai had a chicken diaspora,** and since there are no predators to harm them, their numbers are increasing exponentially.

I look at the Muslims from God's point of view that they are sheep from another sheep pen. We read in John 10:16, **"And I have other sheep that are not of this fold. I must bring them also, and they will listen to my voice. So there will be one flock, one shepherd."**

Since Middle Eastern countries closed their door to missionaries, God caused a tornado in the Middle East that resulted in a **Muslim diaspora** and spread them all over the world, regardless of their intention, so they can be available to hear the gospel of truth from their neighbors in the new country. Muslim populations are increasing in the US with the ratio of four to one, and among them, there are Muslims with bad intentions to destroy this beautiful country from the inside out or convert Americans to Islam through financial incentives, intimidation, or force. **So, our work is cut out for us; either we introduce them to Christ with the light of truth, or they will extinguish our light forever.**

Among the exiled Muslims, there are wolves in sheep's clothing, so-called Muslim evangelists who go into prisons in the United States as Muslim chaplains and attend to prisoners' family needs, especially black families. After they are released from prisons, they are expected to accept Islam as their religion by repeating the Muslim confession (Islamic creed) that Allah is the only god, and Mohammad is his messenger; to put it simply, they are paid to be Muslims. I have come across these Muslims and asked them to make me a Muslim, and I found that they are empty and have no understanding of Islam.

My question is: *What happened to the light of Christ in Christians that people in the US are attracted to the darkness of Islam?*

Jesus said in John 15:5-6 NKJV, "I am the vine; you are the branches. He who abides in Me and I in him, bears much fruit; for without Me you can do nothing. If anyone does not abide in Me, he is cast out as a branch and is withered; and they gather them and throw them into the fire and they are burned."

The church has gone rogue and disconnected from the vine, Jesus, and without that connection, it is rendered useless. Instead of being transformed by the power of the Holy Spirit, the church is conformed to the world around it. The church is supposed to be the torch that is lifted high to be seen by everybody around and shed the light of truth over the darkness, but instead, it is gone dim and, in many cases, dark.

My prayer is that the church becomes the city on the hill which is set aside to be seen by everyone from afar, the city that will shelter its people from the storms of life, and a high tower to run to for protection, peace, and comfort.

I have an Egyptian friend whose wife had heard the gospel from another Egyptian friend of mine, and she accepted Christ as her Savior, got baptized, and her family was totally confused whether to stay Muslim or become Christian. Usually in a Muslim family, we share the gospel with the father, and as he accepts Christ Jesus, the rest of the family will follow, but this time, it was the other way around.

I invited the father and shared the gospel with him, explained the falsehood of Islam, and asked him one question: If the god of Islam is the true god, worship him, but if the Lord Jehovah is the true God, worship Him. A month later, he accepted Christ and got baptized, and after him, the other three children accepted Christ and got baptized.

I was invited to a Baptist church in Texas to give my testimony. The pastor gave me ten minutes to speak because he had to preach. My short-form testimony usually takes half an hour to forty-five minutes, but I was the guest speaker. So, I agreed. I prayed, "Lord I only have ten minutes to glorify Your name, so be glorified." I started my introduction, and five minutes into my testimony, the pastor interrupted me and said that he was not going to preach his sermon; instead, we were going to pray. The Holy Spirit took over the Baptist church, and everybody was on their knees for the next half an hour praying. The Lord received glory, and I received another invitation to teach the church on how to reach out to Muslims for Christ.

My dear fellow humans, the end is near, and the time is running out; evil is on the rise, injustice is everywhere, new world order is upon us, plagues are everywhere and increasing daily, our spiritual and national leaders are confused, lawlessness is rampant, and the love of many has grown cold as Jesus said in Matthew 24:4–14:

> **See that no one leads you astray. For many will come in my name, saying, "I am the Christ," and they will lead many astray. And you will hear of wars and rumors of wars. See that you are not alarmed, for this must take place, but the end is not yet. For nation will rise against nation, and kingdom against kingdom, and there will be famines and earthquakes in various places. All these are but the beginning of the birth pains. Then they will deliver you up to tribulation and put you to death, and you will be hated by all nations for my name's sake. And then many will fall away and betray one another and hate one another. And many false prophets will arise and lead many astray. And because lawlessness will be increased, the love of many will grow cold. But the one who endures to the end will be saved. And this gospel of the kingdom will be proclaimed throughout the whole world as a testimony to all nations, and then the end will come.**

Today a third of the world's population who are Muslims have not heard the gospel of truth, and the Lord is asking the same question that He asked of Isaiah, **"Whom shall I send and who will go for us?"**

As for me, I say: "Here am I lord! Send me"

I truly appreciate the readers of this book who have taken the time to read my story and testimony of how the hand of God worked in my life to bring me out from the darkness of Islam and to the light of Jesus.

I love you from the bottom of my heart, and I have an invitation. Regardless of who you are, Muslim, Buddhist, atheist, or any normal secular human being, we all have sinned and fall short of the glory of God, and if you do not have a personal relationship with God through Christ Jesus, and you are not sure if your sins are forgiven, the Bible has a solution for that in the book of Romans 10:9–13:

> **If you confess with your mouth that Jesus is Lord and believe in your heart that God raised him from the dead, you will be saved. For with the heart one believes and is justified, and with the mouth one confesses and is saved. For the Scripture says, "Everyone who believes in him will not be put to shame." For there is no distinction between Jew and Greek; for the same Lord is Lord of all, bestowing his riches on all who call on him. For "everyone who calls on the name of the Lord will be saved." Amen.**

CPSIA information can be obtained
at www.ICGtesting.com
Printed in the USA
BVHW062203090323
660087BV00020B/998